WHAT CRUCIFIED JESUS?

What Crucified Jesus?

ELLIS RIVKIN

Abingdon Press
Nashville

WHAT CRUCIFIED JESUS?

Library of Congress Cataloging in Publication Data
RIVKIN, ELLIS, 1918–
    What crucified Jesus?
    1. Jesus Christ—Passion—Role of Romans.
    2. Jews—History—168 B.C.–A.D. 135
    3. Rome—Politics and government—30 B.C.–A.D. 68
    4. Jesus Christ—Jewish interpretations. I. Title.
    BT431.6.R58   1984   232.9′6   83-15570

ISBN 0-687-44637-6 (pbk.)

Portions of this book are based on articles by the author: "Who
Crucified Jesus?" *Jewish Heritage* 1/3 (Fall 1958); "Paul and the Parting
of the Ways," *Jewish Heritage* 1/4 (Winter 1959); "Bet-Din, Boulé,
Sanhedrin: A Tragedy of Errors,"*Hebrew Union College Annual* 46
(1975).
    Scripture quotations from the Old and New Testaments are from the
Revised Standard Version of the Bible, copyrighted 1946, 1952, © 1971,
1973 by the Division of Christian Education of the National Council of
Churches of Christ in the U.S.A. and are used by permission.
    Sections from the writings of Josephus are reprinted by permission of
the publisher and the Loeb Classical Library: *Jewish Wars*, Vols. I, II, III,
© 1927, 1928; *Antiquities*, Vols. I, XVIII, XX, © 1930, 1965; *Against
Apion*, Vol. II, © 1926. Harvard University Press.

MANUFACTURED BY THE PARTHENON PRESS AT
NASHVILLE, TENNESSEE, UNITED STATES OF AMERICA

To the memory of Professor Solomon Zeitlin,
who launched me on my odyssey from
Who Crucified Jesus? to *What Crucified Jesus?*

Contents

Preface

I was only a fledgling scholar when Solomon Zeitlin published his *Who Crucified Jesus?* (1942). But even then I was convinced that he had a made a major methodological breakthrough. By setting Jesus' life and ministry securely within the framework of time, place, structure, and circumstance, Professor Zeitlin, it seemed to me, had opened the way for eliciting a credible historical Jesus and a credible trial and crucifixion from recalcitrant sources. Particularly persuasive for me as far as the trial was concerned was Professor Zeitlin's claim that there were two sanhedrins in Jesus' day—one religious, the other political—and that it could have been only the political sanhedrin that tried Jesus.

It is therefore understandable that when, in the course of my research leading to the publication of *A Hidden Revolution*, The Pharisees' Search for the Kingdom Within (Abingdon Press, 1978), I recognized that the writings of Josephus could be used to build an objective framework of time, place, structure, and circumstance for the emergence of a Jesus-like figure; and when I simultaneously discovered that the *bet din* of the Pharisees in Jesus' day was called in Greek a *boulé*, not a sanhedrin (there was a religious *boulé*, but a political sanhedrin), I was impelled to widen the beachhead Professor Zeitlin had established for recovering a credible historical Jesus and a credible trial and crucifixion by drawing upon our sources in an innovative way.

It would have given me great pleasure to dedicate this book to Professor Zeitlin while he was still alive. But since that pleasure is denied me, I would like to dedicate it to the memory of a maverick scholar who embodied the spirit of Torah *li-shemah*, the seeking of truth and knowledge for its own sake, undaunted by fear and impervious to favor—a spirit which is, of necessity, immortal.

Although I am especially indebted to Solomon Zeitlin's work, I am not unmindful of the many other individuals—teachers, colleagues, students, friends, and family—who have influenced my thinking. If I single out only a few, it is simply because of their direct relationship to the finalized manuscript: Professors Shubert Ogden, Victor Furnish, Michael Cook, and Martin Yaffe; Rabbis Jack Bemporad and Mayer Selekman. Each probed the manuscript with the critical eye I so deeply appreciate, though I do not always acquiesce. Peter Obermark and David Williams, graduate Fellows at the Hebrew Union College, were most helpful in many ways; James Kampen and Will Hartfelder, also graduate Fellows, graciously shared their reactions as Christians. Yetta Gershune, through skillful and patient typing of the many manuscript versions, once again demonstrated her commitment to my academic efforts. Nancy Bunker was both gracious and helpful in nurturing the manuscript through the word processor, with generous cooperation from Betty Brady. Dr. Herbert Zafren and his competent library staff were always at hand to facilitate the use of the rich resources of the Hebrew Union College library.

A special word of appreciation is in order for Connie Yaffe, my research associate. She was deeply involved with *What Crucified Jesus?* from its embryonic beginnings to its finished form—always with focused energy, quiet patience, pointed criticism, and a deep appreciation of the problems I was wrestling with.

My indebtedness to my wife Zelda is too deep and too manifold to be diminished by words. Nonetheless, I cannot refrain from expressing my gratitude for her constructive role in helping me reduce an original manuscript of almost three hundred pages to one less than half that length, without either weakening the argument or eliminating any essential data. As for her dedicated collaboration, her ongoing inspiration, and her steadfast love, there is no page that does not bear their imprint.

WHAT CRUCIFIED JESUS?

Who Crucified Jesus?

I t is tragic indeed that the birth pangs of Christianity were occasioned by an event in which Jews were directly implicated. It is tragic because it spawned intense hostility between mother and daughter religions, religions bound by an umbilical cord which can never be severed. As long as the Gospels, Acts, the Epistles of Paul, and the other books of the New Testament are read as holy Scriptures by Christians, the tie to Judaism is a tie that binds. All Christian claims for Christ are grounded in verses from the Old Testament; all Christian claims to be the true Israel are underwritten by proof texts drawn from the Pentateuch; and all Christian claims that Jesus had risen from the dead are embedded in the core belief of the Scribes-Pharisees of Jesus' day. Cut the history and the religion of Israel out of the New Testament, and Christianity vanishes. The Old Testament may be replaced by the New, the Israel of the flesh by the Israel of the Spirit, and the Law by Christ, but the umbilical cord remains.

The umbilical cord remains, yet that tie has been taut with tragedy. Jesus died no ordinary death, in no ordinary circumstances. According to the Gospels, he was arrested by order of the high priest; he was tried before a sanhedrin of Jewish notables presided over by the high priest; he was delivered over to the Roman procurator* by the high priest; he was condemned to crucifixion on the charge of claiming to be the King of the Jews; and he was resurrected by God the Father three days after he had breathed his last. Throughout this horrendous process, Jews are in the forefront: the high priest, scribes and elders, the sanhedrin, the hostile crowd calling for crucifixion, the Jews mocking his royal claim as Jesus hung on the cross twisted and dying. How, on hearing or reading this painful and shocking account of a teacher who had healed the sick, commiserated with the poor, exorcised demons, sat with sinners, and preached of God's coming kingdom, can one respond without pain, sorrow, and bitter anger? And Christians throughout the centuries have responded with pain, with sorrow, and with bitter anger against Jews, who seem to have caused it all.

Crucifixion was a cruel and inhumane act. It would have been cruel and inhumane even were the crucified one guilty of some serious crime. It plumbed the depths of cruelty and inhumanity when it was inflicted on a charismatic, a prophetic

*Although there is evidence that procurator was applied to Roman military governors only from the time of Claudius, and therefore Pilate actually was called prefect of Judea, I prefer to retain the use of the familiar term, since substantively they are synonymous.

visionary, an earnest seeker of salvation and redemption for his people. Those who were ultimately responsible for so heinous a crime are deserving of our righteous wrath, if not of our righteous vengeance.

It is therefore understandable that the disciples of Jesus who witnessed his travail were shocked, outraged, embittered, and unforgiving of those whom they believed to have been responsible. It is also understandable that in the record of Jesus' life, trial, crucifixion, and attested resurrection, there should be so much violent hatred for all those who, in one way or another, had rejected him as the Messiah while he was alive and had rejected him as the Messiah after his disciples had seen him risen from the dead. Were the record otherwise, it would had to have been set down by angels, not beings of flesh and blood.

We cannot therefore shake off this frightening question of responsibility. The New Testament, like the Old, will always be with us. The story will always arouse pain, sorrow, and anger in the hearts of Christians. No surgical procedure can cut away the guts of the Gospel story: an arrest, a trial, a crucifixion, and an attestation to a resurrection.

Nor should we dodge the question of responsibility. As seekers of truth, we would wish to know what occurred, why it occurred, and who was responsible for its occurrence. As seekers of reconciliation between the mother and the daughter religions, we would wish to build this reconciliation on the facing of facts, rather than on the dissolving of them.

13

This twofold goal may perhaps be achieved if we shift our focus from the question, Who crucified Jesus? to the question, *What* crucified Jesus?

But that shifting of focus is more easily suggested than done. For we need some source for Jesus' life that is free of the hostile intensity of the Gospel story—a source that would provide us the historical Jesus, free of the passionate involvement of those who were certain that he had risen from the dead.

But where shall we find such a source? We have only the Gospel record, a record penned with faith, written with passion, and bristling with hostility and resentment. So where are we to turn?

I suggest that we turn to the writings of Josephus— not because he records the life, the trial, the crucifixion, and the resurrection, but because he does not! Josephus was born shortly after Jesus died and was a keen participant and observer of the tumult of the time. As the general in charge of Galilee during the Jews' revolt against Rome, he was actively involved; and he wrote at great length of the road to war, first in *The Jewish War*, then in the last volumes of his *Antiquities*, and finally in his autobiography, *The Life*. As an admirer of Thucydides and Polybius, the grand historians of the Greco-Roman world, Josephus was a penetrative student of political power and a master of historical narrative. As a follower of the Pharisees, he was thoroughly versed in the teachings of the written and the oral Law and was himself a believer in the immortality of the soul and the resurrection of the body. As a committed Jew, he was highly sensitive to the sufferings and helplessness of the Jews pressed

14

in the grip of imperial Rome. Josephus is a precious source, revealing the Roman imperial system as it functioned in Jesus' day; the systems of Judaism prevalent at the time; the revolutionary spasms which convulsed the land; the charismatics, prophets, and would-be messiahs who roamed the hills of Judea and Galilee.

Josephus' work lends itself to the ends we are seeking. From his writings we can construct the framework within which Jesus' life, trial, crucifixion, and resurrection were played out. But we can do even more. With Josephus as our guide, we may be able even to resurrect the historical Jesus who for so long has eluded us. By drawing a portrait of a charismatic of charismatics from the intricate web of time, place, structures, and linkages woven for us by Josephus, we may be in a position to compare this portrait with those drawn for us in the Gospels. Never was the time more ripe or more ready for a spirit capable of charting a trajectory from life to Life—a spirit whose earthly fate would not be his destiny.

Let us then set off on our odyssey from Who crucified Jesus? to What crucified Jesus?—an odyssey from human bitterness, hate, and blindness to divine love, reconciliation, and enlightenment.

2

Render unto Caesar:
In Rome's Imperial Grip

The Jewish people had been in the grip of Rome long before the time of Jesus. From that critical moment when the Roman general Pompey had stamped the seal of Rome on Hyrcanus II (63–40 B.C.), Jews had exercised little control over their land or their destiny. All who governed Jews, whether puppet kings like Herod (40–4 B.C.) or procurators like Pontius Pilate (A.D. 26–36), governed as instruments of the Roman imperium. And Rome's grip loosened not at all in the years that followed the trial and crucifixion of Jesus.

The imperial grip was painful but bearable during those early years when Hyracanus II and Herod retained the trappings of kingly power. It became less and less bearable in the waning years of Herod's reign, and the frustration, the bitterness, and the resentment of the people began to be expressed in strident defiance and violent demonstrations. It became intolerable when, after Herod's death, Rome dispensed with puppet kings and determined to rule Judea directly through procurators appointed by the emperor. From that moment on, the Jews were to know no peace, no serenity, no security until the Temple was in ruins, thousands lay slain, and thousands more had been carted off to Rome.

This epoch of violence was ushered in by an event that occurred on the eve of Herod's death. Some youthful firebrands, stirred by the urgings of two renowned sages, hacked down the golden eagle which Herod had erected over the great gate of the Temple. Apprehended and arrested, they were brought before Herod. When asked by whose orders they had cut down the eagle, they replied, "The law of our fathers." When Herod asked further why they were exultant when death was so imminent, they answered, "Because, after our death, we shall enjoy greater felicity." Enraged, Herod denounced these firebrands before the public assembly as sacrilegious persons who, under the pretext of zeal for the Law, had more ambitious aims in view, and he had them and the sages who had inspired them burnt alive (*Jewish War* I: 648-55).

The anger of the people was not visible at the time of this tragic event. Herod's decision was accepted in silence. But immediately after Herod's death, large numbers gathered in the Temple area and began to bewail the fate of the young men. "This mourning," Josephus tells us,

> was in no subdued tones: there were piercing shrieks, a dirge directed by a conductor, and lamentations with beating of the breast which resounded throughout the

17

city. . . . These martyrs ought, they clamoured, to be avenged by the punishment of Herod's favorites and . . . the deposition of the high priest whom he had appointed, as they had a right to select a man of greater piety and purer morals (*Jewish War* II: 5-13).

All efforts of Herod's son, Archelaus, to still the clamor were of no avail. With Passover at hand, and with the multitudes who were crowding in from the countryside being exposed to the agitations of those mourning for the martyred youths and their teachers, Archelaus was frightened and sent a cohort of troops to suppress the agitators. Indignant at the appearance of the troops, the crowd reacted with violence: They killed most of the soldiers and wounded the tribune in command. Terrified by this show of rebellion, Archelaus ordered his entire army into the city, with the result that three thousand lost their lives while others scattered to the neighboring hills (cf. *Jewish War* II: 5-13).

The cutting down of the eagle, Herod's angry response, the violence of the mourners, and Archelaus' harsh repression of the rioters—all set the stage for the tragedies to come. The golden eagle was an especially sensitive issue. Was it equivalent to an image of the emperor and, as such, an affront to a core belief of Judaism? Or was it merely a symbol of loyalty to Rome? Herod, who viewed the eagle as merely a symbol of loyalty, was outraged. He had always respected the core tenets of Judaism and had demonstrated this respect by rebuilding the Temple in a grand style. How, then, could he be accused of violating the Second Commandment? For him, the eagle was a symbol, pure and simple, and therefore those who were responsible for cutting it down could have been activated only by political motives. But for the two firebrands and their teachers, the golden eagle represented an image of the emperor and, as such, might have been looked upon as an object of divine worship.

The majority of the religious leaders seem to have sided with Herod's view, since they did not challenge his right to execute the troublemakers. As for the people at large, some were so clearly outraged by what Herod had done that they reacted with violent demonstrations. Others may have deplored the execution of the malefactors, even though they themselves looked upon the eagle as an innocuous symbol. The fact, however, that there was no simple way to distinguish religious/nonpolitical action from religious/political action was bound to unleash violent reactions in the years that followed.

Not long after Archelaus had sounded the leitmotiv of violent repression, another fierce confrontation took place between Jews and Romans. A large number of Jews were so angered by the efforts of Sabinus, a Roman officer, to gain access to the royal treasures that they surrounded the Roman troops in the Temple precincts and engaged them in battle. So fierce was their attack that only the reinforcements led by Varus, the governor of Syria himself, finally subdued the outbreak—but not before Varus had set fire to the Temple porticoes. Large numbers of Jews were burned to death in the flames, and still more were butchered by the soldiers. To underscore his determination to dampen the Jews' passion for violent confrontations with Roman authority, Varus *crucified* about two thousand of the most active insurrectionists and imprisoned a large number of the "less turbulent" (*Jewish War* II: 66-75).

At the time these disruptive events were occurring, other upheavals were also disturbing the peace. In Galilee, Judas, the son of Ezechias, a revolutionary from Herod's day, "raised a considerable body of followers, broke open the royal arsenals, and, having armed his companions, attacked the other aspirants to power" (*Jewish War* II: 55-56).

Not to be outdone, in Peraea, a certain Simon crowned himself, perambulated the country with a band of revolutionaries, and burned down the royal palace at Jericho, along with many other stately mansions. "Not a house of any respectability," writes Josephus, "would have escaped the flames," had not Gratus, the commander of the royal infantry, decapitated Simon in a hand-to-hand encounter (*Jewish War* II: 58-59).

Another aspirant to the throne, a shepherd by the name of Athrongaeus, donned a diadem and led raiding expeditions throughout the country. His victims, according to Josephus, were not only Romans and royalists, but any wealthy Jews who had the misfortune to fall into his clutches. Only with difficulty did the authorities apprehend the leaders of these bandits (*Jewish War* II: 60-65).

And while all this turbulence was rocking Judea, the Emperor Augustus was giving ear to the various contenders for Herod's mantle and pondering whether Judea should continue to be governed by a puppet king, as Herod had been, or by a direct appointee from Rome. Augustus finally opted for direct rule. He reduced the territory of Archelaus, Herod's son, to a Roman province and sent out Coponius, a Roman of the equestrian order, to serve as procurator. He was invested with full powers, including that of inflicting capital punishment.

Coponius ushered in the new dispensation with an act that set the teeth of the Jews on edge. No sooner had he taken office than he ordered a census and an assessment of Jewish property, in order to determine the amount of tribute to be exacted. The Jews were shocked and inclined to resist. Only the pleas of the high priest deterred them from what would have been a tragic confrontation. But two sages, Judas of Galilee and Zadok, a Pharisee, refused to knuckle under. They called on the people to revolt, insisting that God and God alone could be called *despotes*, Emperor. It was blasphemous, they said, to obey the Roman emperor's decrees. "Heaven would be their zealous helper," they reassured the people, "to no lesser end than the furthering of their enterprise until it succeeded—all the more if with high devotion in their hearts they stood firm and did not shrink from the bloodshed that might be necessary" (*Antiquities* XVIII: 5-6).

The appeal of Judas and Zadok did not go unheeded. Indeed, so many flocked to their banner that they fathered within Judaism a Fourth Philosophy, alongside the three philosophies already in existence—those of the Sadducees, the Pharisees, and the Essenes. Though adhering to Pharisaic teachings on all other issues, the followers of the

Fourth Philosophy rejected the dictum of the Pharisees that the law of the emperor was to be obeyed as long as it did not violate any of the core teachings of Judaism.

Josephus tells us that the Fourth Philosophy attracted many followers. He also assures us that "these men sowed the seed of every kind of misery, which so afflicted the nation that words are inadequate [and that] when they had won an abundance of devotees, they filled the body politic immediately with tumult, also planting the seeds of those troubles which subsequently overtook it, all because of the novelty of this hitherto unknown philosophy" (*Antiquities* XVIII: 6; 9-10).

The rise of the Fourth Philosophy underscores the blurred line that separated the religious/nonpolitical realm from the religious/political realm. From the point of view of the founders of the Fourth Philosophy, the call for revolution against Rome was inspired by religious, not political zeal. They claimed that it was blasphemous to call any individual *despotes*, lord, master, emperor. God and God alone was *despotes*, Lord, Master, Emperor. Their call to arms was intended to overthrow another Antiochus who was challenging God's claim to be the only God. Such a call to arms had political consequences, but it was not motivated or justified on political grounds. The fact that both Judas and Zadok were sages, not soldiers, and the fact that Josephus dignified this revolutionary movement by setting it beside the schools of thought of the Sadducees, Pharisees, and Essenes as another

22

religious philosophy within Judaism attest to the religious wellsprings of this violent challenge to Rome.

From the point of view, however, of the High Priest Joazar and from the point of view of the leading spokesmen for the Pharisees, the taking of a census, the assessment of property, and the payment of tribute fell within Caesar's domain. For them, paying tribute to the emperor was not equivalent to paying tribute to a god.

Thus when Pontius Pilate entered on his procuratorship in A.D. 26 and immediately reconfirmed Caiaphas as high priest, he fell heir to a country that had been wracked by continuous violence from the moment the youths had torn down the golden eagle. Judea was clearly no sinecure. It was, rather, a battleground where the mettle of the procurator and his high priest was put to the test day-in and day-out. If Pontius Pilate were to make his mark and show himself worthy of advancement in the hierarchy of imperial power, it was essential that he impress the emperor with his ability to maintain law and order in a land which had proven itself to be a seedbed of dissidence, disorder, and violence. Tiberius (A.D. 14–37), who had succeeded Augustus as emperor and had appointed Pilate, was scarcely in the mood for a repetition of the years of turbulence that had shaken Judea after the death of Herod. Unless, then, Pontius Pilate were shrewd enough to govern this unruly people, his tenure as procurator was bound to be extremely short.

The nub of Pontius Pilate's problem was where to draw the line between the legitimate rights of the

Jews to exercise religious autonomy—rights which the Roman emperors themselves had granted—and the illegitimate stretching of those rights to the point at which they became religious justifications or pretexts for challenging Roman authority. Such a line, however, was not an easy one to draw. Was the Roman eagle a symbol of loyalty to Rome, or was it an object of worship? Were the Jews merely demanding their religious rights when they equated the golden eagle with busts of the emperor, or did their objection mask a political challenge, thinly veiled by a religious pretext?

Whereas the affair of the golden eagle did not lend itself to easy categorization, the ideology of the Fourth Philosophy offered no such ambiguity. From the outset, Judas of Galilee and Zadok the Pharisee had made no bones about the political consequences of their insistence that only God could be called *despotes*. Even though this insistence was religious in appeal and motivation, it could not be acted upon without defying Roman political authority. One who heeded the religious call of Judas and Zadok must refuse to pay taxes to Rome, an act of disobedience which the Romans could not possibly allow to be disguised as an appeal to religious autonomy. Furthermore, since their defiance went hand in hand with a call for a violent uprising against the Romans and their Jewish collaborators, there was no question that the followers of the Fourth Philosophy had crossed the line that separated religious from political turf.

Pontius Pilate, confronted as he was with the need to make tough decisions, and concerned as he was with exacting the required tribute, needed to impress the people with his toughness and yet avoid the need for force majeure. He therefore gingerly experimented with a point where he might safely draw the line. His first experiment was a failure; the second was a success. Here is Josephus' account of Pilate's first test of the people's mettle:

Pilate, being sent by . . . Tiberius as procurator to Judea, introduced into Jerusalem by night and under cover, the effigies of Caesar which are called standards. This proceeding, when day broke, aroused immense excitement among the Jews; those who were on the spot were in consternation, *considering their laws to have been trampled underfoot,* as those laws permit no image to be erected in the city; while the indignation of the townspeople stirred the country folk, who flocked together in crowds. Hastening after Pilate to Caesarea, the Jews implored him to remove the standards from Jerusalem and to uphold the laws of their ancestors. When Pilate refused, they fell prostrate around his house and for five whole days and nights remained motionless in that position.

On the ensuing day Pilate took his seat on his tribunal in the great stadium and summoning the multitude, with the apparent intention of answering them, gave the arranged signal to his armed soldiers to surround the Jews. Finding themselves in a ring of troops, three deep, the Jews were struck dumb at this unexpected sight. Pilate, after threatening to cut them down, if they refused to admit Caesar's images, signalled to the soldiers to draw their swords. Thereupon the Jews, as by concerted action, flung themselves in a body on the ground, extended their necks, and exclaimed that they were ready rather to die

25

than to transgress the law. Overcome with astonishment at such intense religious zeal, Pilate gave orders for the immediate removal of the standards (*Jewish War* II: 169-174; emphasis mine).

However, Pilate's second experiment proved more successful:

On a later occasion, he provoked a fresh uproar by expending upon the construction of an aqueduct the sacred treasure known as *Corbanas* [Greek transliteration from the Hebrew word meaning *sacrifices*]; the water was brought from a distance of 400 furlongs. Indignant at this proceeding, the populace formed a ring around the tribunal of Pilate, then on a visit to Jerusalem, and besieged him with angry clamour. He, foreseeing the tumult, had interspersed among the crowd a troop of soldiers, armed but disguised in civilian dress, with orders not to use their swords, but to beat any rioters with cudgels. He now from his tribunal gave the agreed signal. Large numbers of the Jews perished, some from the blows which they received, others trodden to death by their companions in the ensuing flight. Cowed by the fate of the victims, the multitude was reduced to silence (*Jewish War* II: 175-77).

It is evident that Pilate's sacrilegious act angered the people. It is also evident that they did not regard this sacrilege as one that must be resisted by martyrdom. Pilate as a plunderer of the Temple treasury was guilty of outright robbery and disrespect, but he was not guilty of imposing idolatrous

26

images upon the Jews. Hence his show of strength was sufficient to cow Jewish resistance.

Pontius Pilate and the people at large thus, early on, knew where they stood with each other. Pilate had been forewarned that any tampering with an *essential* belief of the Jewish people would be resisted with martyrdom. On the other hand, if his provocations fell short of such tampering, the people would give way to coercive pressure.

It is evident from Josephus' account that Pontius Pilate was shrewd, tough, ruthless, and successful. His ten years in office testified to his good record in the preserving of law and order. He was able to head off trouble before it reached dangerous proportions. *His key to effective governance was to nip revolutions in the bud by making no distinction between "political" and "religious" dissidents. Dissidence, not motive or rallying cry, was his target.* For him, a charismatic's vision of the kingdom of God as one that God himself would usher in was equally as threatening as the revolutionaries' call to rise up against the Romans, for the end result would be the same: Roman rule would be finished. For Pilate, the beginning of wisdom was the fear of revolt, however masked by religious pietudes.

But Pilate could not achieve his objectives unless there were a loyal and able Jewish counterpart as committed to Pilate's strategy as was Pilate himself. In Caiaphas, he found such a counterpart. No previous high priest had ever held this high office for such a long period of time, and no subsequent high priest was ever to best Caiaphas' record. This was no mean achievement. Every procurator, both prior to and following Pontius Pilate, was free to employ a pliant high priest. Since Herod's day, the high priest had been appointed and dismissed at the whim of the ruler. The high priest's sacred robes were kept under lock and key by the political authorities, to be released only on festivals when he needed them in order to perform his duties. *Held thus firmly in the grip of puppet king or procurator, all high priests had to toe the line.*

Yet Caiaphas seems to have been the only high priest who possessed those special qualities which enabled him to serve not just one, but two procurators. Since he held the office for a full ten years under such a demanding procurator as Pontius Pilate, Caiaphas obviously had the ability to keep the anger of the people from boiling over into violent anti-Roman demonstrations. This was no easy task, when we bear in mind that it was Caiaphas who was the high priest when Pilate aroused the wrath of the people by bringing the effigies of the emperor into Jerusalem, and also when he robbed the Temple treasury to build an aqueduct. Yet Caiaphas weathered the storms and held his post throughout Pilate's administration. No major disturbances marred their relationship—an eloquent testimony to the high priest's skill in snuffing out sparks before they burst into flames.

There was one event, however, during the high priesthood of Caiaphas, which reveals the fear and trembling in high places. Although this event occurred outside the political jurisdiction of Pontius Pilate, it reflects the cast of mind of all who exercised authority during those discordant and troublesome times. It involved a charismatic, John the Baptist, who was put to death by Herod the Tetrarch.

Here is Josephus' account of the occurrence and of the motives that prompted the ruler's violent reaction:

But to some of the Jews the destruction of Herod's army seemed to be divine vengeance, and certainly a just vengeance, for his treatment of John, surnamed the Baptist. For Herod had put him to death, though he was a good man and had exhorted the Jews to lead righteous lives, to practice justice towards their fellows and piety towards God, and so doing to join in baptism. In his view, this was a necessary preliminary if baptism was to be acceptable to God. They must not employ it to gain pardon for whatever sins they committed, but as a consecration of the body implying that the soul was already thoroughly cleansed by right behaviour. When others too joined the crowds about him, because they were aroused to the highest degree by his sermons, Herod became alarmed. *Eloquence that had so great an effect on mankind might lead to some form of sedition*, for it looked as if they would be guided by John in everything they did.

Herod decided, therefore, that it would be much better to strike first and be rid of him before his work led to an uprising, than to wait for an upheaval, get involved in a difficult situation and see his mistake. Though John, because of Herod's suspicions, was brought in chains to Marchaerus, a [stronghold], and there put to death, yet the verdict of the Jews was that the destruction visited upon Herod's army was a vindication of John, since God saw fit to inflict such a

29

blow on Herod (*Antiquities* XVIII: 116-119; emphasis mine).

Josephus had little sympathy for Jews who sought to overthrow Roman rule. Yet he was not at all pleased with rulers who provoked the people unnecessarily by clamping down on religious zealots and ardent preachers, especially when, as in the case of John, their preaching was aimed at stirring the people to cleanse themselves of their sins—not of their rulers. John, in Josephus' opinion, was a good man who exhorted the Jews to live righteous lives, to practice justice toward their fellows and piety toward God. When John called the people to join him in baptism, he was urging them to participate in a symbolic act signifying that their souls had already been cleansed by the righteous lives they had lived since heeding his call. There was nothing political in John's teachings. He was a religious charismatic—pure and simple.

Yet as Josephus points out, Herod the Tetrarch was unwilling to accept John for what he was. As long as crowds were aroused by John's sermons, the ruler feared that such eloquence could stir the people to some form of sedition. For John was no ordinary preacher. He could so stir his listeners with his aura that they would willingly follow wherever he might lead. Thus Herod was confronted with a dilemma: If he ignored John, the crowds might become more and more prone to violence in response to some real or imagined provocation. On the other hand, if he put John to death, he might be inviting the very outbreak he was attempting to avoid. It turned out that, in this instance at least, Herod the Tetrarch had made a shrewd decision: The people, though aroused and angry, did not rise up.

The Roman imperial framework, within which Jesus' life, preaching, trial, crucifixion, and attested resurrection took place, is clear enough. At the pinnacle of power and authority was the emperor, who exercised his authority over the Jews either through puppet kings, like Herod, or through procurators, like Coponius and Pontius Pilate. These imperial instruments, in turn, sought to carry out their responsibilities to the emperor by appointing high priests, who were selected for their pliancy rather than their piety. Their function was to serve as the eyes and ears of the puppet king or procurator, so as to head off demonstrative challenges to Roman rule. Of these high priests, only one—Caiaphas— had such piercing eyes and such keen ears that he was able to keep the confidence of the procurators he served as long as they remained in office.

But even Caiaphas could scarcely have done his job single-handedly. It is thus highly likely that he appointed a council, or sanhedrin, consisting of individuals who were well aware of the dire consequences that would follow any outbreak against Roman authority, however innocent and naive its instigator. To be sure, such a sanhedrin is not specifically mentioned by Josephus in his account of the incumbency of Pontius Pilate and Caiaphas. But he does mention such a sanhedrin when he tells us of the trial and stoning of James, the

brother of Jesus, during the procuratorship of
Albinus and the high priesthood of Ananus:

> The younger Ananus, who . . . had been appointed to
> the high priesthood, was rash in his temper and
> unusually daring. He followed the school of the
> Sadducees, who are indeed more heartless than any of
> the other Jews . . . when they sit in judgment.
>
> Possessed of such a character, Ananus thought that
> he had a favourable opportunity because Festus was
> dead and Albinus [the new procurator] was still on the
> way. And so he convened a sanhedrin of judges and
> brought before them a man named James, the brother of
> Jesus who was called the Christ, and certain others. He
> accused them of having transgressed the law and
> delivered them up to be stoned.
>
> *Those of the inhabitants of the city who were*
> *considered the most fair-minded and who were strict*
> *in the observance of the law were offended at this.*
> They therefore secretly sent to King Agrippa urging
> [that he order Ananus] to desist from any further
> actions. Certain of them even went to meet Albinus,
> who was on his way from Alexandria, and informed
> him that Ananus had no authority to convene a
> sanhedrin without his consent. Convinced by these
> words, Albinus angrily wrote to Ananus threatening to
> take vengeance upon him. King Agrippa, because of
> Ananus' action, deposed him from the high priesthood
> which he had held for three months and replaced him
> with Jesus the son of Damnaeus (*Antiquities* XX:
> 197-203; emphasis mine).

Josephus' account of the stoning of James is of
vital importance, for it reveals the role of the high

32

priest as being that of the procurator's procurator. It also reveals the thin line that separated the religious from the political realm. Ananus, Josephus tells us, was a high priest and a Sadducee. Taking advantage of the brief period when there was no procurator in Jerusalem, Ananus acted as though he himself were the procurator. He not only convened a sanhedrin, but he had James stoned to death on the grounds that he had violated the law. This act, however, aroused such bitter opposition from those who were strict in their observance of the laws— the Scribes-Pharisees*—that they informed King Agrippa of Ananus' illegal action. Others reminded Albinus that *Ananus had no right to convene a sanhedrin in the absence of the procurator.* Whereupon King Agrippa lost no time in deposing Ananus from the high priesthood.

The striking point here is that Ananus was a Sadducee. He thus could not possibly have seen eye to eye with the Pharisees on matters of religious law. The Sadducees believed that God had revealed the written Law only, while the Pharisees taught that God had provided for two Laws, a written Law *and* an oral Law. *The Pharisees could not have participated in a sanhedrin if a judgment were to be made on the basis of religious law, even though they could participate in a sanhedrin if the basis of judgment were to be political.*

---

*After much research I am convinced that although in the Greek and Roman translations of the Gospels they are treated as referring to separate classes, the terms *Scribe* and *Pharisee* are synonymous. (See Rivkin, "Scribes Pharisees Lawyers, Hypocrites: A Study in Synonymity," *Hebrew College Annual* 49 [1978]).

James' preaching may have been deemed politically dangerous by the high priest, even though the message was couched in religious language. *But James' preaching clearly was not deemed political by the strict observers of the religious laws, the Pharisees.* They were appalled at Ananus' harsh and illegal judgment and took steps to have him removed from office.

Throughout this passage, Josephus assumes that the sanhedrin which Ananus convened was a sort of privy council, not a permanent body which enjoyed a religious status independent of the high priest and procurator. It is thus evident that, whatever the religious commitments of the members of this council may have been, when they served on the high priest's council, they served as political, not religious advisors.

That the sanhedrin was a privy council and not a religious body is further confirmed by Josephus when he recounts the episode in which Agrippa granted the Levites the right to wear linen garments, as did the priests:

> The Levites . . . who were singers of hymns urged the king to convene a Sanhedrin and get them permission to wear linen robes on equal terms with the priests. . . . The king, with the consent of those who attended the sanhedrin, allowed the singers of hymns to discard their former robes and to wear linen ones such as they wished. A part of the tribe that served in the temple were also permitted to learn the hymns by heart, as they had requested. All this was contrary to the ancestral laws, and such transgression was bound to

34

make us liable to punishment (*Antiquities* XX: 216-18; We are dealing here with a break from custom, not law, since Levites are *not* prohibited from wearing linen. At the same time, there was no law which, as was the case with the priests, commanded them to wear linen. But as students of religion know only too well, any deviation from a traditional mode or practice can wound religious sensitivities, even when such a deviation is not from law, but from precedent and custom.).

It is evident from our reading of Josephus that King Agrippa had the right to convoke a sanhedrin—a privy council—to advise him with respect to an issue that lay within his *political* jurisdiction—that is, the Temple and its management. *We are therefore not dealing with a sanhedrin that possessed some permanent religious or political status, but rather with a privy council that functioned as an adjunct to the political authority.*

Indeed, when Josephus uses the term *sanhedrin* in his writings, *it always refers to a council appointed by an emperor, a king, or a high priest.* He never uses the term when he is speaking of a permanent legislative body such as the Roman Senate. Such a body, he usually calls a *boulé*. Thus whenever Herod wished to have one of his sons, wives, or other relatives put to death for treason, he would convoke a *sanhedrin*, not a *boulé*. Such a sanhedrin based its judgment on political, not religious grounds. Similarly, when Josephus tells us of Herod's trial and uses the term *sanhedrin*, it is because Herod was being tried for overstepping his political, not his religious authority. Sameias and Pollion, both Pharisees, participated in that sanhedrin, but they were sitting on a sanhedrin as powerful leaders concerned with *political* issues, *not* as religious leaders intending to judge Herod on religious grounds.

Although Josephus does not specifically mention that Caiaphas convoked a sanhedrin, this does not mean that Caiaphas did not have a privy council; for Josephus says nothing about Caiaphas' priesthood, other than that he was the high priest. We may therefore assume that if Caiaphas had had to deal with a charismatic such as Jesus, he would have been unwilling to render a judgment without taking counsel with a sanhedrin, his privy council, which had only a political, not a religious function.

A close reading of Josephus has provided us with the political framework within which the life, ministry, trial, crucifixion, and witnessed resurrection of Jesus were played out. This is the framework presupposed by the Gospels, by Acts, and by the Epistles of Paul. The Roman emperor ruled Judea, Galilee, and Samaria by means of puppet kings, governors, procurators, and procurator-appointed high priests. But the Jewish people over whom these instruments ruled proved to be ungovernable.

In such a world, where violence stalked the countryside, death frequented the streets of Jerusalem, and riots disturbed the precincts of the Temple; where every flutter of dissidence sent chills of fear up the spines of puppet kings, governors, procurators, and procurator-appointed high priests—even the most nonpolitical of charismatics took his life in his hands when he preached the good news of God's coming kingdom. And if his call to repentance were so eloquent that crowds gathered round to hear and to hope, would not the power of his word invite the kiss of death?

3

Render unto God:
The Mosaic of Judaism

Judea was under the control of Rome. The emperor, the procurator, the high priest, and the high priest's privy council—all were tied together by two interests: the preservation of imperial power in the face of any challenge, and the smooth collection of tribute for the enrichment of Rome. All those who functioned in the imperial interest were not motivated by religious, but by political considerations. The high priest was no exception, even though he ministered in the Temple, and he alone was allowed to enter the Holy of Holies on the Day of Atonement to seek God's forgiveness for the sins of all Israel. Yet he himself was, in the sight of God, an arch sinner, for nowhere in the five books of Moses or in the repository of the oral Law, the Mishnah, do we read that a high priest is to be an appointee of any king, prince, or potentate. According to the Pentateuch, the high priesthood was to be reserved for the direct lineal descendants of Aaron, Eleazar, and Phineas.

From the standpoint of God's Law, all high priests who had held office since Herod's day were illegitimate. They had been merely political instruments imposed by regal power and acquiesced to by the leaders of the three divergent forms of Judaism in Jesus' day—the Judaism of the Sadducees, of the Pharisees, and of the Essenes. Though the followers of each of these forms regarded the followers of the others as heretics and rejectors of God's will, Judaism appeared to the Roman authorities as a mosaic with three inlays, which, though distinguishable one from another, were nonetheless of a single design. And this was so because, out of desperation, the leaders of each form had committed themselves to two doctrines: the doctrine of the two realms to regulate their relationship to the state, and the doctrine of live and let live to regulate their relationship to one another. In a word, they urged their followers to render unto Caesar what was Caesar's, so that they would be able to render unto God what was God's. And they also, in order to exist amiably side by side with one another, had initiated a policy of peaceful coexistence.

Let us now take a closer look at each of the three inlays—the Sadducees, the Pharisees, and the Essenes—so that we can comprehend how three such divergent forms of Judaism could have appeared to the Roman authorities as a mosaic, rather than as separate, distinct, and mutually exclusive forms of the religion of Israel. For at first glance, the differences that set them apart were far more impressive and fundamental than those that drew them together.

The Sadducees believed that God had revealed one Law only—the five books of Moses; the Scribes-Pharisees believed that God had revealed two Laws—one written and the other oral; while the Essenes believed that God had also revealed his will in books besides the Pentateuch and the other books of the Bible. There were additional significant differences as well: The Sadducees believed that God had endowed Aaron and his sons with absolute authority over God's Law and over his cultus; the Scribes-Pharisees believed that God had endowed first Moses, then Joshua, then the elders, then the prophets, and then themselves with absolute authority over God's twofold Law, the written and the oral; while the Essenes kept themselves aloof from the people at large and from the cultus of the day. And finally, while the Sadducees believed that God rewarded the righteous and punished the wicked in this world, the Scribes-Pharisees believed that God rewarded the righteous with eternal life for the soul and resurrection for the body and that he punished the souls of the wicked with eternal suffering in the nether world. As for the Essenes, they believed that the souls of the righteous would enjoy eternal life, but they did not believe in the resurrection of the body. But however severe and tenacious the differences, Sadducees, Scribes-Pharisees, and Essenes all looked to God, not to the Roman emperor as their Lord. Whereas the procurator-appointed high priest and his privy council were harnessed to the imperial chariot, the Sadducees, Pharisees, and Essenes were yoked to God.

In Jesus' day the Scribes-Pharisees were the most luminous inlay within the mosaic of Judaism. It was they who sat in Moses' seat, and it was they who determined the norms by which all public religious functions were carried out in accordance with the provisions of the written and oral Law. Thus the religious calendar of the Temple followed the lunar-solar calendar of the oral Law. The sacrifices in the Temple and the celebrations of the festivals were carried out in accordance with the oral Law. In a word, the oral Law of the Scribes-Pharisees was normative for all Jews, insofar as public manifestations of religion were concerned. The religious activity of the Sadducees and Essenes was confined to their private domains, and their religious teachings were restricted to doctrinal claims and verbal protestations.

It had not always been thus. The Scribes-Pharisees had not always sat in Moses' seat. In fact, they had been sitting there only since the Hasmonean revolt (167–142 B.C.). Before that time, the Scribes-Pharisees had not even existed—those in authority had belonged to the Aaronide priesthood, presided over by a high priest who traced his descent from Aaron, Eleazar, Phineas, and Zadok. The Aaronide priesthood had administered the written Law. The rewards and punishments they proclaimed to the people were this-worldly. Their religious calendar was not geared to the moon, but to the sun. All public worship was carried out precisely as Moses had prescribed in the Pentateuch. No other class either had or sought authority over the Law. The scribes in those days had been intellectuals who pursued Wisdom, not power, and they heaped praises on the high priest and his fellow-Aaronides. They were not the Scribes-Pharisees of Jesus' day.

These Scribes-Pharisees were newcomers. They had burst out in response to the crisis which Antiochus Epiphanes precipitated when he launched his drive to hellenize and polytheize the Jews. By expelling Onias II from the high priestly office and exiling him to Egypt, and by appointing first Jason and then Meneleus in his stead, Antiochus had violated the provisions laid down by the Pentateuch for the high priestly succession. And by his insistence that, on pain of death, Jews must worship Zeus and abandon their God-given laws, Antiochus compelled them to weigh the consequences of martyrdom, since the Pentateuch confined rewards and punishment to this world. If one obeyed the Law, one died; if one disobeyed, one lived. Thus in the train of these events, there opened up a leadership gap and a doctrinal gap—gaps which the Scribes-Pharisees jumped in to bridge.

They bridged the leadership gap by seating themselves in Moses' seat, and they bridged the doctrinal gap by proclaiming that God had given two Laws, the written and the oral—not the written only; and that God had promised eternal life for the soul and resurrection for the body to each individual who adhered to this twofold Law. Martyrdom would not end in death, as the Pentateuch implied, but in life eternal.

42

Many years after this good news was proclaimed by the Scribes-Pharisees, Josephus held up this belief as the great prize which awaited every Jew who loyally adhered to the twofold Law:

> For those who live in accordance with our laws the prize is not silver or gold, no crown of wild olive or of parsley or with any such public mark of distinction. No; each individual, relying on the witness of his own conscience and the lawgiver's prophecy, confirmed by the sure testimony of God, is firmly persuaded that those who observed the laws and, if they must need die for them, willingly meet death, God has granted a renewed existence and in the revolution of the ages the gift of a better life.
>
> I should have hesitated to write thus, had not the facts made all men aware that many of our countrymen have on many occasions ere now preferred to have all manner of suffering rather than utter a single word against the law (*Against Apion* II: 218-19).

Josephus pictures the glorious life after death of the righteous in another passage:

> Know you not that they who depart this life in accordance with the law of nature and repay the loan [of the soul] which they received from God, when he who lent is pleased to reclaim it, win eternal renown; that their houses and families are secure; that their souls, remaining spotless and obedient, are allotted the most holy place in heaven, whence in the revolution of the ages, they return to find in chaste bodies a new habitation?
>
> But as for those who have laid mad hands on themselves [and committed suicide], the darker regions

of the nether world receive their souls, and God, their father, visits upon their posterity the outrageous acts of the parents (*Jewish War* III: 374-75).

That the souls of the deserving will enjoy the nearness of God the Father is foreshadowed by the words Josephus puts in Abraham's mouth as the Patriarch readies himself to sacrifice his son Isaac:

"Aye, since thou wast born (out of the course of nature, so) quit thou now this life not by the common road, but sped by thine own father on the way to God, the Father of all, through the rites of sacrifice. He, I ween, accounts it not meant for thee to depart this life by sickness or war, or by any of the calamities that commonly befall mankind, *but amid prayers and sacrificial ceremonies would receive the soul and keep it near to Himself;* and for me thou shalt be a protector and stay of my old age—to which end above all I nurtured you—by giving me God in the stead of thy self."

The son of such a father could not but be brave-hearted, and Isaac received these words with joy (*Antiquities* I: 228-32; emphasis mine).

This was good news indeed. God the Father loved each and every individual so much that he had revealed his two-fold Law to Israel, so that each individual who internalized this Law and adhered to it could look forward to eternal life for the soul and resurrection for the body. Uplifted by teachings as intoxicating as these, the overwhelming majority of the Jewish people gladly followed the teachings of the Scribes-Pharisees and happily acknowledged their right to sit in Moses' seat.

Not so the previous Aaronide leaders. They denounced this new class of Scribes as *perushim* (*pharisaio* when transliterated into the Greek; hence the English *Pharisees*)—that is, *separatists, deviants, heretics*. When, in 142 B.C. a Great Synagogue invested Simon the Hasmonean with the high priesthood even though he was not a direct descendant of Aaron-Eleazar-Phineas-Zadok, the old priestly leaders proclaimed that only a Zadokite could be allowed to serve as high priest. The high priestly Aaron-Eleazar-Phineas line had been spelled out by Moses himself, and from the time Zadok had served as high priest in Solomon's Temple, the high priesthood had been exclusively the prerogative of his descendants. Those who justified a break from this line were violators of God's Law, for nowhere in the Pentateuch is a Great Synagogue mentioned, much less authorized to seat or unseat a high priest. Those who justified a non-Pentateuchal body, and those who justified the investiture of a non-Zadokite as high priest on the grounds of an oral Law, could not be *soferim* (respected scribes as Ben Sira had been), but were usurpers, separatists, deviants, *pharisaio*—guilty of defying the clear, plain, and unambiguous words written down by Moses at God's command. Those who resisted the claims of this class came to be called the Zedukkim—that is, Sadducees.

The Sadducees' denunciations, however, were not heeded by the overwhelming majority of the Jewish people. For them, the good news of eternal life and resurrection preached by the Scribes-Pharisees proved far more alluring than the literal reading of Scripture by the Sadducees. Therefore, from the time of their triumphant ascendancy during the Hasmonean revolt until the time of Jesus and beyond, the Scribes-Pharisees sat securely in Moses' seat. Even when John Hyrcanus (135–105 B.C.) broke with the Pharisees and abrogated the oral laws, the mass of people clung to the Scribes-Pharisees. And when Alexander Janneus (102–76 B.C.) persisted in negating the oral laws, the people at large rose up in violent revolt and refused to give in until Salome Alexandra (76–67 B.C.) reinstituted the oral laws and restored the Scribes-Pharisees to their dominant role. Aside from this violent interlude, the oral laws of the Scribes-Pharisees, called halakha in Hebrew, spelled out the norms by which all public manifestation of religion was conducted and by which the majority of Jews regulated their personal lives.

Although neither John Hyrcanus nor Alexander Janneus succeeded in their efforts to break the power of the Pharisees, they did succeed in forcing them to come to terms with the realities of political and religious power. Having suffered the brutalities of civil war and fearing such strife as a way of life, the Scribes-Pharisees were ready to accommodate themselves to the stubborn realities of this world by according recognition to the state as an independent entity, and by according the Sadducees and the Essenes exemption from the provisions of the oral Law, insofar as this-worldly sanctions were concerned. This twofold accommodation to the specter of civil war was made manifest in the two doctrines mentioned: the doctrine of the two realms and the doctrine of live and let live.

Let us take a closer look at the way these doctrines evolved and functioned during the latter years of Hasmonean rule and beyond. As for the doctrine of the two realms, having suffered grievously from the indecisive civil war throughout the reign of Alexander Janneus, the Scribes-Pharisees had a strong interest in a peaceful settlement with the Hasmoneans. Although under Salome Alexandra the Pharisees once again enjoyed a degree of political power, by the end of her reign they came to recognize that the political arena was not their stage—that they were religious teachers whose power came from their preaching of the good news of eternal life and resurrection and from the love and respect they inspired in the masses. Convinced that this world was transient and that earthly satisfactions were of little moment, they focused their minds on the world to come, which would be eternal and fully satisfying.

Since the trappings of worldly power had no hold over them, the Scribes-Pharisees were willing to make a compact with their rulers, a compact which would accord to each realm its due. If the political authorities would agree to recognize the right of the Scribes-Pharisees to teach the twofold Law, determine the norms of public manifestations of religion and the liturgical calendar, and preach the good news of eternal life and resurrection, then the Scribes-Pharisees, for their part, would acknowledge the right of the political authorities to impose taxes, raise armies, fight wars, and administer the nonreligious areas of economic, social, and political life. In a word, the Scribes-Pharisees enunciated the doctrine of the legitimacy of two realms, the secular and the religious.

This doctrine proved to be attractive to the secular/political authorities. Thus they were willing to grant religious autonomy to the Scribes-Pharisees. The implications of this doctrine, however, were to have momentous consequences; for it meant nothing less than a promise on the part of the Scribes-Pharisees that as long as their religious autonomy was not violated, the political authorities were to be given a free hand.

This compact had its beginnings during the reign of Salome Alexandra. It was crystalized and activated after her death when the Scribes-Pharisees withdrew from the political arena. It was sustained throughout Herod's reign and reinforced when the procurators took over. In confirming the right of the procurator to collect tribute, the Scribes-Pharisees were translating their doctrine of the two realms— from rendering unto the king what is the king's and unto God what is God's, to its new formulation: Render unto Caesar what is Caesar's and unto God what is God's.

The doctrine of the two realms thus proved to be an eminently satisfying solution for the Scribes-Pharisees. They could more and more wash their hands of dirty politics, palace intrigues, and repressive measures, to concentrate on saving souls. Even when they were consulted by the political authorities, the responsibility for decision making lay squarely in the hands of those authorities and not in the hands of the Scribes-Pharisees. Such decisions were political, not religious. Scribes-Pharisees were consulted only because they had the trust of the people and could be counted on to fulfill their end of the contract—remind their followers that the secular rulers must be obeyed as long as they did not obstruct the road to eternal life and resurrection.

This the Scribes-Pharisees could do with a clear conscience. Their teachings had never promised the people a garden of roses in this world—only in the world to come. God's justice could not be weighed and measured by earthly felicity or by earthly pain and suffering. Indeed, without trials and tribulations, how was God to distinguish the sturdy righteous from those whose righteousness waxed and waned with the rewards and punishments of each passing day? Suffering, whether at the hands of the Hasmoneans, at the hands of the Herodians, or at the hands of the procurators was thus no justification for either revolt or for railing at God's unconcern. Rather, it was a challenge to one's faith, a trial of one's beliefs, and a goad to one's righteousness. Suffering must be endured with resolute patience and stoic calm as long as the political authorities did not close off the glory road to everlasting life.

But should the political authorities fail to stay within their realm, should they trespass on the realm of the holy and sacred, then the people must rise up in revolt, as they had done when John Hyrcanus and Alexander Janneus had barred the road to eternal life. Or they could resort to passive resistance, willing to martyr themselves rather than yield. This they had indeed done when they refused to be cowed by Pontius Pilate's threats if they persisted in blocking the introduction of the emperor's images into Jerusalem and into the Temple.

The doctrine of the two realms proved to be a fruitful one. The political rulers, whether Hasmoneans, Herodians, or Romans, treated the Scribes-Pharisees with respect and, with the rarest of exceptions, did not obstruct their teachings, or tamper with their laws, or threaten their institutions. Thus Herod had released two Pharisaic sages, Sameias and Pollion, along with their disciples, from the need to take a loyalty oath to him. Contrariwise, Herod appealed successfully to the leaders of the Scribes-Pharisees when the firebrands tore down the golden eagle. Similarly, the most prestigious Pharisees were called upon by the political authorities to urge the people not to revolt against Rome even after the provocations of the procurator had become intolerable (*Jewish War* II: 411-14). All these instances bespeak a trust: The Scribes-Pharisees would keep their side of the contract as long as the political rulers kept theirs.

This compact was reaffirmed when Coponius, having been appointed procurator after Herod's death, ordered the census to serve as the basis for the exaction of the imperial tribute. This order, as we have seen, was so bitterly resented by the people that it could easily have sparked a revolt, had not the Scribes-Pharisees stood firmly behind their compact. The exaction of tribute fell in Caesar's domain.

It did not bar the road to eternal life. The census-taking was a legitimate exercise of Roman authority and could not be challenged on religious grounds, no matter how much suffering and hardship the exaction of tribute would impose upon the people. The census was legal, the tribute was legal, its exaction was legal because Roman sovereignty was legal. It was legal because the doctrine of the two realms accorded to Caesar all that was Caesar's and to God all that was God's.

The Scribes-Pharisees' adherence to their compact was not without heavy cost. For the first time since they had taken possession of Moses' seat, they found their leadership rejected by a significant number of their followers when Judas and Zadok denounced Coponius' order as being an affront to God's sovereignty. So fundamental indeed was this split with the Scribes-Pharisees that the Fourth Philosophy came to be recognized as a distinctive form of Judaism, alongside those of the Scribes-Pharisees, the Sadducees, and the Essenes.

As for the doctrine of live and let live, the Scribes-Pharisees of Jesus' day had long since given up their earlier efforts to bind the Sadducees to the oral Law. Except for worship in the Temple, adherence to the religious calendar, and conformance to public ceremonial acts of a religious and public nature, the private acts and teachings of the Sadducees and their followers had come to be regarded as their own affair. Conflicts between Scribes-Pharisees and Sadducees were now confined exclusively to doctrinal debate. On a day-to-day basis, Scribes-Pharisees and Sadducees mingled freely, and Sadducean high priests carried out their Temple functions in accordance with the prescriptions of the oral laws with seeming good grace. Indeed, on such issues as political sovereignty, the Scribes-Pharisees and Sadducees tended to see eye to eye, since the Sadducees, like the Scribes-Pharisees, had committed themselves to the doctrine of the two realms. As long as the political authorities did not violate the fundamental principles of the written Law that there is only one God, that no image of that God may be worshiped, and that sacrifices be offered up to God in his holy Temple, then as far as the Sadducees were concerned, there could be no challenge to the right of the political authorities to impose taxes, maintain law and order, and even to keep the garments of the high priest under lock and key.

So, too, the Scribes-Pharisees and Sadducees had agreed to a similar binding compact which regulated their relationship to each other. As long as the Sadducees carried out all public functions in accordance with the oral Law, the Scribes-Pharisees would raise no question to the right of a Sadducee to be a high priest; or to the right of Sadducees to be priests and to enjoy all the honors, privileges, and revenues attendant to their priestly status; or to live their private lives outside the jurisdiction of the oral Law. The ultimate judgment was transferred from the hands of men to the hands of God. If, as the Scribes-Pharisees taught, God will punish with eternal suffering those who reject the twofold Law, the Sadducees would receive the punishment they deserved in the world to come. For their part, the

Sadducees could anticipate that God would punish the Scribes-Pharisees for their heretical teachings by shortening their lives, visiting on them pain and suffering, withholding prosperity, and denying them the blessings of children in this world.

As long, then, as the ultimate sanctions were left to God, it was possible for Scribes-Phrarisees and Sadducees to limit their doctrinal conflicts to acerbic debate. In many areas of mutual concern, especially those that might endanger the very existence of the people and the sanctuary, they could even collaborate. Of these areas, the most sensitive was the grey and murky area which lay between the religious realm and the political realm. For it was in this area that religious dissidence could not always be distinguished from political challenge—yet on this distinction, the life and death of the people hung precariously.

As for the Essenes, they, too, were subsumed under the compact of live and let live. As long as they kept to themselves and made no effort to gain control over the Temple cult, the Scribes-Pharisees and Sadducees were willing to let God decide what was to become of them.

It is thus evident that in Jesus' day, the Scribes-Pharisees and the Sadducees coexisted peacefully on the religious plane and held similar views on the political plane. Both had adopted a noninterference policy, not only toward each other, but toward every religious group in Judaism, however much it might deviate from their own beliefs. Whatever common concern they shared over religious dissidents whose teachings had dangerous political implications, such concern was political, not religious: Dissidents should be brought before some appropriate political authority—puppet king, procurator, or procurator-appointed high priest—to be judged on political grounds. Such dissidents were not brought before the Bet Din Ha-Gadol (Great Boulé), the senate of the Scribes-Pharisees, or before any of their lesser bodies, each of which was called simply a *bet din (boulé)*. In Jesus' day, these bodies did not exercise any political jurisdiction, while the religious jurisdiction they did exercise was limited to those Jews who voluntarily followed the teachings of the Scribes-Pharisees. Adhering to their compact with the state, the Scribes-Pharisees steered clear of political involvement; and adhering to their compact with the Sadducees and Essenes, they confined their outrage at religious dissidents to verbal onslaughts. If, then, a charismatic stirred crowds with his call for repentance, awed crowds by his wonder working, or uplifted crowds with the promise of God's kingdom to come, then the Scribes-Pharisees might confront him, they might remonstrate with him, they might even denounce him as an emissary of Beelzebul, but they would not—*for they could not*—arrest him and have him brought before either the Bet Din Ha-Gadol, or a lesser *bet din*. They could no more haul a charismatic before their religious bodies than they could haul the High Priest Caiaphas, who, as a Sadducee, held far more outrageous religious beliefs than those held by many of the charismatics.

Thus the Judaism in Jesus' day, though it consisted of three distinctive facets blended together, appeared to the Romans as a mosaic, rather than as separate and distinct insets. For though the Scribes-Pharisees, Sadducees, and Essenes looked upon one another as religious heretics, they all adhered to the doctrine of the two realms and the doctrine of live and let live. The Romans could therefore be certain that as long as they did not compel the Scribes-Pharisees, Sadducees, or Essenes to worship the emperor as a god, or to install busts of the emperor in the Temple; and as long as the Romans did not interfere with their right to teach their distinctive doctrines, the leaders, whether of the Scribes-Pharisees, of the Sadducees, or of the Essenes, would urge their followers to be loyal to Rome, pay the tribute, and resist the blandishments of revolutionaries and charismatics—however couched in prophetic and pietistic language those blandishments might be. For the Romans, then, these three distinctive forms of Judaism formed a mosaic which flashed from all its facets the reassuring message: "Render to Caesar the things that are Caesar's, and to God the things that are God's" (Mark 12:17).

4

From out of the Depths
They Cried

The mosaic of Judaism was not fractured by the provocations of the ruling authorities. But many Jews found those provocations so painful that they could not submit passively. For them, the situation demanded some alternative to the doctrine of the two realms. It was inconceivable to them that God could be party to such harsh injustices. They believed that God could not and would not remain silent. Although the Pharisees, Sadducees, and Essenes may have drawn a line between the religious and secular realms, God had drawn no such line. Voices began to cry out that God was not neutral and that Caesar's realm was neither safe nor sacrosanct. They believed that God's righteous justice would not be deterred by some imaginary line drawn by men—that God would bring low the haughtiness of emperors and wreak vengeance on their cruel injustices to God's people. Some believed the wrath of God would be manifested through violent revolutionaries. For others, God's wrath required no human instruments of violence; these people were drawn to charismatic teachers who proclaimed that the peaceful kingdom of God was at hand.

Those who were stirred to take the extreme revolutionary road had been inspired by the two sages, Judas of Galilee and Zadok the Pharisee, who, as we have seen, had been aroused by the refusal of the Pharisaic leaders to regard the census as a religious issue and by their refusal to denounce the tribute. For Judas and Zadok, the issue was a religious one. They must throw down the gauntlet and take up arms against Rome. In this battle, God surely would lend power to those who were championing his cause and assure them victory.

This call to arms did not go unheeded. Many desperate Jews rallied around Judas and Zadok, confident that God was *not* neutral and that he would bless their violence with victory. These revolutionaries and their Fourth Philosophy gave the Romans and their Jewish collaborators no peace until their lives and their violence were snuffed out at Masada in the year A.D. 71.

The followers of the Fourth Philosophy, by rejecting the doctrine of the two realms, aroused the opposition not only of the Romans and their puppet high priests, but also of the Pharisees, to whom they previously had been attached and to whose other doctrines they still adhered. But there was this difference: The Roman authorities and their Jewish surrogates countered violence with violence, while the Scribes-Pharisees confined their hostility to verbal denunciation and villification. The Scribes-Pharisees exercised no coercive authority in the secular realm. Their authority was limited to public manifestations of religion—the liturgical calendar and the Temple ritual. Otherwise they adhered to their policy of noninterference. Sadducees and Essenes were not subjected to the *bet din*, the *boulé*, of the Scribes-Pharisees, even though they rejected the twofold Law, and the same tolerance was extended to the Fourth Philosophy. Once Judas and Zadok broke from the Scribes-Pharisees, they were out of the jurisdiction of Pharisaic institutions. However much the Scribes-Pharisees may have denounced these leaders, however much they may have viewed the deaths of their followers at the hands of the Romans as a retribution from God, they themselves confined their hostility to verbal denunciations.

For the Roman authorities and the high priest, the Fourth Philosophy offered no real problem as to how it should be dealt with, since its followers made no bones about their determination to overthrow Roman rule by force. Every effort to root them out, therefore, was deemed justified. Violence must be met with violence. The religious justification for their revolutionary ideology mattered neither to the Roman procurators nor to the high priests. As long as the Romans did not set up statues of the emperors in the Temple or parade icons of the emperor through the streets of Jerusalem, they felt that no Jew had the right to arouse the people to challenge Roman rule on religious grounds. As far as the procurators and the high priests were concerned, the line of demarcation between the realm of Caesar and the realm of God was a line which both God and the emperor had drawn.

It was not so easy, however, for the authorities to decide what to do about charismatic leaders who preached no violence and built no revolutionary organizations, but rather urged the people to repent and to wait for the coming of God's kingdom. Were these charismatics harmless preachers, or were they troublemakers? Were their teachings and visions goads to personal righteousness, and therefore apolitical or even nonpolitical? Or were they goads to dissatisfaction and unhappiness with the world that was?

The prophetlike charismatics were preachers, not revolutionaries. They resembled the prophets of old. They did not call upon the people to rise up against Rome, but to look to God, who had the power to perform miracles and move mountains. One such charismatic, Theudas, attracted vast crowds of credulous believers who followed him toward the Jordan River, anticipating that God would split the Jordan for him as certainly as it had been split for Joshua—only to have their hopes dashed when Roman soldiers apprehended Theudas and put him to death.

A similar fate befell another prophetlike redeemer—this one from Egypt. He was, according to Josephus, a charlatan who had gained the reputation of a prophet. This man appeared in the nation, collected a following of about thirty thousand, and led them by a circuitous route to the Mount of Olives. From there he proposed to force an entrance into Jerusalem and, after overpowering the Roman garrison, to set himself up as a tyrant of the people. His attack, however, was anticipated by the procurator, Felix, who went to meet him with the Roman infantry. The outcome of the ensuing engagement was that the Egyptian escaped with a few of his followers; most of his force was killed or taken prisoner; the remainder was dispersed and stealthily escaped to their several homes (*Jewish War* II: 261-63).

Josephus chose Theudas and the Egyptian false prophet out of a seething prophetic brew. They were but two examples of the charismatics who flourished alongside the dagger wielding Fourth Philosophers, also called the Sicarii. Josephus describes them as follows:

A new species of banditti [sprang] up in Jerusalem, the so-called *sicarii*, who committed murders in broad daylight in the heart of the city. The festivals were then special seasons, when they would mingle with the crowd, carrying short daggers concealed under their clothing, with which they stabbed their enemies. Then, when they fell, the murderers joined in the cries of indignation and, through this plausible behavior, were never discovered. The first to be assassinated by them was Jonathan the high-priest; after his death there were numerous daily murders. The panic created was more alarming than the calamity itself; everyone, as on the battlefield, hourly expecting death. Men kept watch at a distance on their enemies and would not trust even their friends when they approached. Yet, even while their suspicions were aroused and they were on their guard, they fell; so swift were the conspirators and so crafty in eluding detection (*Jewish War* II: 254-57).

Josephus gives us a feeling for the kind of chaos and anarchy that was prevalent and the kind of emotional and psychological disorientation that followed in its wake. He was not concerned with cataloguing an exhaustive list of charismatics. He selected a Theudas here, an Egyptian false prophet there as illustrative examples. He felt no need to name every prophetlike figure who stirred the people with visions of redemption. As a historian, he wished to convey the fact that suffering, distress, and disorientation had made the soil fertile for the resurrection of the spirit of prophecy, a spirit that had been so prominent in former days when suffering, distress, and disorientation had been dealt out by imperial powers. This resurrection of the prophetic spirit was, for Josephus, a frightening specter. Like his Pharisaic teachers, he believed that prophecy had come to an end with the death of Malachi. He looked on this outburst of prophetic fervor as fraudulent and dangerous—so much so, in fact, that he calls the perpetrators "deceivers and imposters . . . with purer hands but more impious intentions," and claims that they were no less responsible than the outright assassins for ruining the peace of Jerusalem.

Yet amid this cacophony of prophetic and charismatic voices, there were some that Josephus himself recognized as arising from sincere, righteous, and benign teachers, calling upon the people to turn their hearts and minds to God and repent of their sinful ways. He heard their calls for repentance not as calls for arms or even for miraculous deliverance, but rather as calls for religious renewal, calls which no follower of the Scribes-Pharisees could gainsay.

One such charismatic was John the Baptist. Josephus' vignette of John is so essential for the thesis of this book that a portion of it is worthy of reiteration:

> *He was a good man and had exhorted the Jews to lead righteous lives, to practice justice towards their fellows and piety towards God. . . . When others too joined the crowds about him, because they were aroused to the highest degree by his sermons, Herod [the Tetrarch] became alarmed. Eloquence that had so great an effect on mankind might lead to some form of sedition, for it looked as if they would be guided by John in everything he did. Herod decided therefore that it would be much better to strike first and be rid of him before his work led to an uprising, than to wait for an up-heaval, get involved in a difficult situation and see his mistake. . . . The verdict of the Jews was that the destruction visited upon Herod's army was a vindication of John, since God saw fit to inflict such a blow on Herod* (Antiquities XVIII: 116-19; emphasis mine).

Josephus' brief account is of striking value. It illuminates an obscure and murky landscape: the turf where religious claims to autonomy and Roman claims to sovereignty could not easily be differentiated. *There was no way to predict whether a pious charismatic's call for repentance would have unintended political consequences.* For most Jews, John was simply a preacher of righteousness whose teachings were free of political intent. John was calling for righteous lives, just actions, and pious commitments—not for a revolt against Rome. His baptism was no cleansing for battle against Caesar, but the mark of a battle against sin already won. Nor was John dangling the prospect of miracles that would transform the earthly world, but miracles that would transform the world within. Therefore when the people learned that Herod Antipas had put John to death, they were appalled. Then when Herod's army was destroyed, they were gratified that the death of the goodly John had been avenged. Josephus is thus only summing up the attitude of a follower of the Scribes-Pharisees when he describes John as a good man who preached the righteous life so eloquently that his cruel death was worthy of being avenged by God himself.

Josephus' portrayal of John reveals that there could indeed be a charismatic teacher whose teachings were nonpolitical but could arouse fear in the hearts of the authorities, who were concerned only with the thought that the crowds gathering round him might get out of control and go on a rampage. Thus Herod the Tetrarch deemed it "better to strike first."

James, the brother of Jesus, was another apolitical preacher who was put to death by the High Priest Ananus, to the dismay of those strict observers of the Law—the Scribes-Pharisees. In his account, Josephus' sympathies are clearly with James and those "inhabitants of the city who were considered the most fair-minded and who were strict in observance of the law"—those who were offended by the high priest's highhandedness in convoking a sanhedrin in the absence of the procurator and in putting James to death (*Antiquities* XX:197-203).

Several issues here disturbed Josephus. First, there was the matter of jurisdiction, since Ananus had no right to convoke a sanhedrin on his own authority. The high priest was the political appointee of the procurator and as such, could not carry out an execution without the express approval of the procurator. Hence when Ananus took the law into his own hands, it was recognized as a breach of his authority. The responsible leaders in Jerusalem immediately sent a message to Agrippa II, alerting him of Ananus' illegal actions. Others went directly to the procurator Albinus and informed him that Ananus had convened a sanhedrin without the procurator's consent. Outraged, Agrippa deposed Ananus from the high priesthood.

Second, although Ananus' action might have been prompted in part by his loyalty to the Sadducees in attempting to find a way to execute James, *the instrument that he used for this purpose—a sanhedrin—was a political, not a religious body.* Since Ananus had no authority to convene a sanhedrin without the procurator's consent, such a council had no religious function. This is confirmed by the fact that the strict observers of the Law, the Scribes-Pharisees, were so aroused that they immediately took steps to have Ananus ousted. *It was not Ananus' displeasure with James' beliefs, but his abuse of political authority that so outraged them. Ananus had used a political instrument, a sanhedrin, to rid himself of a religious dissident.* If Ananus had been allowed to get away with this breach of legality, he might at some future time have been tempted to use his political authority against the Scribes-Pharisees themselves.

Josephus' brief account of the reaction to the trial and execution of James reveals that religious dissidence was not viewed by the Scribes-Pharisees as sufficient justification for political repression. Political repression was allowable only to the degree that certain religious teachings might represent a clear and present political danger, a danger the Scribes-Pharisees obviously did not consider to have been represented by James' teachings. But it must be added that if there had a been a clear and present danger, it still was not the high priest's place to make such a judgment on his own authority. The procurator alone had the ultimate responsibility for determining whether a dissident was or was not politically dangerous.

Josephus' account has another importance—an importance that scholars have tended to overlook. This is the only time Josephus mentions Jesus in a passage whose authenticity has never been challenged. Yet in this one passage, Josephus tosses out Jesus' name only parenthetically, so as to establish James' identity. *Nonetheless, by doing so, Josephus reveals that Jesus must have been well known to his readers.* In order to make clear to the reader the reason for the fuss and fury over James, Josephus merely points out that James was the brother of "Jesus called the Christ." Clearly, no further explanation was necessary, since every cultured Greek and Roman who might read Josephus' *Antiquities* would have known about the Christians. They thus would have understood immediately why James and his associates had been arrested, brought before a sanhedrin, and executed. After all, had that not happened to Jesus himself, the brother of James? *The single word* Christ *used by Josephus was thus sufficient to account for all that had happened.* It was not James who was on trial, but his preaching that Jesus, the Christ, had risen from the dead—a claim that would especially arouse the wrath of a high priest who was a Sadducee. It would also help to explain why "the strict observers of the Law" were incensed. For though the Scribes-Pharisees may not have believed that Jesus was the Christ and had risen from the dead, they wanted no Sadduceean high priest bringing the Pharisaic belief in resurrection into question. We need only recall how Paul provoked a clash between Pharisees and Sadducees when he was brought before a sanhedrin and cried out, "Brethren, I am a Pharisee, a son of Pharisees; with respect to the hope and the resurrection of the dead I am on trial" (Acts 23:6).

Josephus' testimony is revealing also because it makes clear that he did not believe James deserved death on the grounds of having preached the risen Christ. It makes clear, too, that the "strict observers of the Law" did not regard James' preachings as dangerous. Even though they themselves were loyal to Rome, they did not hesitate to let King Agrippa and Albinus know that they disapproved of what Ananus had done.

It is thus evident from Josephus' writing that there were influential Jews who drew a line between outright revolutionaries who called for the overthrow of Rome in God's name, and charismatics who, like John the Baptist, called upon the people to repent; or who, like James, the brother of Jesus, preached the risen Christ. They saw no danger to Rome in religious preachings that looked to God, rather than to arms for salvation. Even though, in the case of James, these Jewish leaders rejected the claims that Jesus had risen from the dead, they still observed their doctrine of noninterference. God, not men, would be the ultimate arbiter. As Gamaliel, the Scribe-Pharisee, is reported to have said to the high priest's sanhedrin: "Keep away from these men and let them alone; for . . . if it is of God, you will not be able to overthrow them" (Acts 5:38-39). Surely, since the Sadducees daily preached outright rejection of the Pharisaic belief in the resurrection, and the Scribes-Pharisees lifted no finger to harm them, then James, who acknowledged the Pharisaic belief in the resurrection each time he proclaimed Jesus as risen from the dead, should be left to God's judgment, not man's.

Josephus' testimony as to the state of affairs in Jesus' day is now spread before us. There were the Sadducees, Pharisees, and Essenes who adhered to the doctrine of the two realms and to the doctrine of live and let live. They had made their peace with Rome and with themselves. But alongside them were those revolutionaries who sought to overthrow Roman rule by force and those prophetlike charismatics who preached repentance and God's redemptive power. The reactions of these two groups to the harshness of Roman rule clashed with the passive acquiescence of the Sadducees, Scribes-Pharisees, and Essenes. The Fourth Philosophy could not insulate religious beliefs from political consequences, while the charismatics, advocating no violence, could delude themselves into thinking that as long as it was God, not men, who swept out Roman rule, the authorities might regard their preaching as devoid of political implications.

The Roman authorities, however, made no distinction. To them, revolutionaries and charismatics alike were outside the mosaic of Judaism. They all preached novel doctrines which set them apart from the Sadducees, Scribes-Pharisees, and Essenes. The charismatics were politically dangerous because their teachings and eloquence attracted crowds—and crowds were unpredictable and therefore dangerous. Charismatics, prophets, visionaries—all were potentially threatening and therefore better out of the way. The line between the two realms, insofar as the authorities were concerned, was clearly and sharply drawn. It was a line of demarcation which separated the mosaic of Judaism from those deviations that flowered from the seeds of violence which the emperor, the procurator, and the high priest had sown.

In the Likeness
of the Son of Man

Amid the spiritual convulsions of those troubled times, and amongst the prophetlike preachers and charismatics who were crying out the good news that God would soon redeem his people from bondage, we scan the writings of Josephus in vain for that charismatic of charismatics whom we would have anticipated finding there—a charismatic so compassionate, so loving, so eloquent, and so filled with the Spirit of God that his disciples would refuse to accept his death as real. But Josephus shares with us only the charismatic John the Baptist. Yet, for all his charisma, John the Baptist failed to arouse in his disciples a love intense enough or a faith secure enough to evoke his death as but a prelude to life. However overwhelmed with grief, and however drawn to his person John's disciples may have been, they did not see him risen from the dead, even though the Scribes-Pharisees were daily preaching resurrection, just as they daily reaffirmed it when they recited the Tefillah, the prayer par excellence, as required by the twofold Law. John's charisma, however impressive and alluring, clearly lacked the power to sustain his life beyond the grave.

The sound, the fury, and the tumult of the times cry out for a charismatic of charismatics. Yet Josephus gives us no such unique individual. He readies us for a Jesus, but gives us only John the Baptist. His fleeting allusion to Jesus as the brother of James fades away as he concentrates on James' fate, not Jesus' resurrection. Josephus' awareness that Jesus was called the Christ, that James must have preached him as risen from the dead, remains unarticulated. For whatever reason, Josephus bespeaks John the Baptist, not Jesus called the Christ.

Josephus' silence stimulates us to try our own hand at painting a portrait of the missing charismatic of charismatics from the pigments of the age which Josephus has preserved in his palette. We ask ourselves: What manner of man would such a charismatic have been? What qualities must he have had to so endear himself to his disciples that even death itself did not have the power to pry them apart? What must his likeness have been to so entrance his followers that they were open-eyed to see his likeness, as much alive after death as before? In a word: What qualities must this unique individual have possessed to make him an even more powerful and alluring charismatic than John?

For an individual to succeed in winning so devoted a following, he must have had fused within himself the wonder working charisma of an Elijah, the visionary power of an Isaiah, the didactive persuasion of a Pharisaic sage. But he must have been more than a mere fusion of such guiding spirits. To outlive death itself, he would have had to *feel* the sufferings of the poor, *experience* the humiliation of the degraded, *sense* the loneliness of the outcast, *taste* the despair of the sinner, and *envelop* all who came within his shadow with his graciousness, compassion, and undemanding love.

He would, in addition, have had to exhibit all the commanding characteristics of the great prophets of action—Moses, Samuel, Elijah, Elisha. Those prophets had been bold leaders, impressive wonder-workers, and freely accessible to the people at large. They had spoken simply, directly, and forcefully. They had acted fearlessly and decisively. Chosen by God to be his servants, there could be no flinching or turning back for any one of them. Whatever the hardship, whatever the pain, whatever the disappointment, their steadfast loyalty to God had never wavered.

Of all the prophets, Elijah would have had a special attraction for a charismatic of charismatics. Elijah, more than the other prophets of action, was of folklike hue. He had been a ruggedly austere man of God, yet his heart had overflowed with compassion. He had championed Naboth's cause when Ahab sought to confiscate the good man's vineyard. He had wrought miracles, bringing back to life the child of a good and simple woman who had offered him hospitality. He had stood up to King Ahab and heaped God's curses upon him, had challenged the prophets of Baal and brought them low. He had drifted about from place to place, a sojourner in his own land, had sought refuge in a cave with only the still small voice of God to reassure and comfort him. It wasyhe alone of all the prophets who had been whirled upward into heaven in a blazing chariot drawn by horses of fire (II Kings 2:11, cf. 2:10), and it was he alone whom God had assigned a special role in ushering in the great and terrible day of the Lord (Malachi 4:5).

Though for the charismatic of charismatics, Elijah would stand out most vividly, other prophets of action—Moses, Samuel, Elisha—would also have served as models. All had been charismatics; all had been fearless leaders; all had been endowed with wondrous power. "In troubled times such as these," he would wonder, "might not God raise up a prophet who would resemble a Moses, a Samuel, an Elijah, or an Elisha—one who would work wonders and lead the people out of their distress?"

Our charismatic of charismatics would have had, in addition to the great prophets of action, the grand visionary prophets to inspire him. Of these, Isaiah and Ezekiel were especially prominent. Isaiah had pictured a glorious end of days when the leopard would lie down with the lamb and swords would be beaten into ploughshares; when a shoot would come forth from the stump of Jesse, and a branch would grow out of his roots, and the Spirit of the Lord would rest upon him:

73

The spirit of wisdom and understanding,
the spirit of counsel and might,
the spirit of knowledge and the fear of the LORD.

(Isaiah 11:2)

No other prophet etched so sharp an image of a messianic figure as did Isaiah—or so attractive a vignette of human fulfillment. For a charismatic of charismatics, the Anointed One of the stump of Jesse would be the Messiah, the model ruler, who

shall not judge by what his eyes see,
or decide by what his ears hear;
but with righteousness he shall judge the poor,
and decide with equity for the meek of the earth. . . .
Righteousness shall be the girdle of his waist,
and faithfulness the girdle of his loins.

(Isaiah 11:3b-4, 5)

The age the Messiah ushered in would be one in which

the leopard shall lie down with the kid,
and the calf and the lion and the fatling together,
and a little child shall lead them.
The cow and the bear shall feed;
their young shall lie down together;
and the lion shall eat straw like the ox.
The suckling child shall play over the hole of the asp,
and the weaned child shall put his hand on the
adder's den.
They shall not hurt or destroy
in all [God's] holy mountain;
for the earth shall be full of the knowledge of the LORD
as the waters cover the sea.

(Isaiah 11:6-9)

For a charismatic of charismatics, this vision would have been a prophecy emanating from God and therefore bound to come to pass at the end of days.

This absolute trust in Isaiah's prophecy would have been reinforced by all the other prophets who had spun out visions of the end of days. The visions of Ezekiel with their picturings of the fury and tumult that would herald God's coming; the quickening of the dead; the restoring of the people of Israel to a renewed life under a beneficent shepherd of the house of David—all would have a powerful attraction. God had addressed Ezekiel also as Son of man, an elusive designation and one that could have aroused in a charismatic of charismatics the notion that *Son of man* might designate a person as being more than a prophet. Perhaps it was the name God would give his Anointed, when the kingdom was finally at hand.

And then there was Malachi, who envisioned the end of days as coming on the heels of Elijah's return to earth, when he would "turn the hearts of fathers to their children and the hearts of children to their fathers" (Malachi 4:6).

A man able to fuse an Elijah with an Isaiah— behaving like the former and dreaming like the latter, being both a wonder-worker and a visionary—would indeed be fit for the role of charismatic of charismatics. He would mingle with the poor and lowly and revive their spirits with his spirit. He would stir them with hope and faith as he proclaimed that the kingdom of God was coming. He would look very much like a prophet of olden times, but he would also bear the likeness of the Son of man, the Anointed, the King-Messiah, ushering in the day of the Lord. He would have stamped on his countenance the image of an Elijah, the image of an Isaiah, and the fused image of the Son of man as both prophet and King-Messiah.

In addition to these, he would have fused within himself the model of a Scribe-Pharisee. This image would have been sui generis, for it would have been that of a teacher who *taught* the Word of God, not that of a prophet who *spoke* the Word of God. Unlike the prophets, the Scribes-Pharisees never prefaced their teachings with "Thus saith Yahweh," even though what they taught—the Halakha (oral Law) and the Aggadah (oral lore)—was deemed to be even more authoritative than that which had been uttered by even the greatest of prophets, Moses himself. The laws that God had commanded and which Moses had written down in the Pentateuch had been subordinated to the oral Law of the Scribes-Pharisees; while the moral and ethical injunctions that God had revealed to Moses and to the prophets were themselves dependent upon the meaning assigned them by the Scribes-Pharisees.

The Scribe-Pharisee was thus cut from a very different cloth than the prophet of old. The Scribe-Pharisee was preeminently a teacher, around whom disciples flocked and at whose feet they sat. Like the Stoic sage, the Scribe-Pharisee walked about with his disciples and freely discoursed on the oral and written Law and on the oral and written lore. Legal opinions mingled freely with reflections on God, Torah, Israel, and the struggle of the individual to subdue the power of sin so as to gain the bliss of the world to come. His discourses on Law and lore were punctuated with deftly chosen proof texts from the Pentateuch, the Prophets, and the Hagiographa, giving their words the assured ring of divine authority by linking the written with the oral Law. The Scribe-Pharisee roamed Scripture, searching for verses, words, even letters, which would become grist for his mill. Whatever meanings his own dicta required from these verses, words, and letters, he elicited with flair and confidence.

Venerated and respected by the people at large, the Scribe-Pharisee taught with authority, but an authority that was collective, not individual. It derived from being a bona fide teacher of the twofold Law—a teacher who, in Jesus' day, was a follower of either the school of Hillel or the school of Shammai. The time had not yet come when he was authorized to expound oral laws in his own name. This had to wait for the destruction of the Temple in A.D. 70. He was not yet called rabbi, *my teacher*, but only rab, *teacher*. As a teacher, he was an expositor of the twofold Law as agreed to by the scholar class as a whole, or as expounded by the school with which he was affiliated.

But whether the Scribe-Pharisee were a follower of the school of Hillel or the school of Shammai, he was a devotee of the twofold Law and a firm believer in eternal life for the soul and resurrection for the body. He also was committed to the doctrine of the two realms and to the doctrine of live and let live. As such, he would be highly skeptical of would-be messiahs who dangled before the suffering masses the illusory hope of God's coming kingdom. The Scribe-Pharisee would be especially hostile toward any individual who claimed a singular authority derived from a special relationship to God and who looked upon himself as the Son of man or the King-Messiah. Such an individual would provoke the Scribe-Pharisee, who would challenge the would-be Son of man in debate, deride him before multitudes, even denounce him as Beelzebul's emissary. *But he would not drag him off to a bet din (boulé) of the Scribes-Pharisees, any more than he would drag there a Sadducee who derided belief in the twofold Law and resurrection.*

A charismatic of charismatics would nonetheless have been very much attracted to the leadership style of the Scribes-Pharisees. Indeed, at first glance, he would so resemble them that it would be difficult for the Scribes-Pharisees themselves to distinguish him from a teacher of the twofold Law. For like them, he would be a speaker, not a writer—an expositor of Law and lore who drove home his teachings with parables and paradigms and a sprinkling of illuminating proof texts. Even the substance of his teachings would frequently echo those of the Scribes-Pharisees: He would proclaim God's Oneness; call on the people to love God with all their heart and being; urge his listeners to love their neighbors as themselves; acknowledge the legitimacy of Caesar's realm; and trumpet the good news of eternal life and resurrection. But when he spoke of a special relationship to God the Father; or flirted with the idea that he might be the Son of man; or exorcised demons; or displayed miraculous powers of healing; or spoke of God's kingdom as being at hand; or edged toward looking upon himself as the King-Messiah, his resemblance to a Scribe-Pharisee would fade away. The Scribes-Pharisees would reject any seeming likeness of the charismatic of charismatics to a Pharisaic sage. They would call so aberrant a teacher to task for leading the people astray with his delusions and would denounce his claims as spurious.

A charismatic of charismatics would thus appear to be an amalgam of three venerated leadership types: the prophet of action, the prophet of vision, and the Scribe-Pharisee. Depending upon what he was teaching or doing at any given moment, and depending upon who was listening to him, he would seem to be now an Elijah, now an Isaiah, now a Scribe-Pharisee. But the decisive point would not be the likenesses—however powerful and alluring they might be—but the goodness, the compassion, the gentleness of soul which reached out with caring love to the lowly, the disheartened, the dispirited. Only qualities such as these could bind those whom he touched with cords of love and faith, cords so taut that even death could not relax them. It was not the fusing of an Elijah, an Isaiah, and a Scribe-Pharisee into his person—these alone would not have rendered him deathless; perhaps even John the Baptist may have effected such a fusion—but his healing and loving spirit, which had the power to restore souls to life.

If such a charismatic had taught and preached during the years when Pontius Pilate was procurator and Caiaphas was high priest, what would his fate have been? None other, we can be sure, than the fate that had overtaken John the Baptist. If such a charismatic were believed to be an Elijah when he healed the sick, raised the dead, and cast forth demons, his wonder working would have attracted crowds—and crowds, as we know, were dangerous and could get out of hand. If he seemed to be a visionary and, like Isaiah, proclaimed that the kingdom of God was near at hand, his high hopes would have attracted crowds—and crowds, as we know, were dangerous and could get out of hand. If he bore a likeness to the Son of man, the King-Messiah, his likeness would have attracted crowds—and crowds, as we know, were dangerous and could get out of hand. And if his compassion and love reached and lifted up the wretched, gave hope to the outcast, and reassurance to the faint of heart, such compassion and love would have attracted crowds—and crowds, as we know, were dangerous and could get out of hand.

Crowds were dangerous indeed! So dangerous, in fact, that Herod the Tetrarch had put John the Baptist to death—not because John urged the people to repent, live pious lives, and undergo baptism, but only because his eloquence attracted crowds and crowds were unpredictable and prone to violence. Ever since the young firebrands had torn down the Roman eagle in God's name, violence had become a nomal response to Roman provocation. Even the presence of Roman legionnaires in the Temple precincts could not deter crowds from going berserk.

What chance for survival would a charismatic of charismatics have—this man of eloquence, wonder-works, religious fervor, fevered fantasies, messianic pretensions, and sheer charisma—if his person attracted crowds in Jerusalem, where Pontius Pilate and his high priest Caiaphas quaked at every rustle of discontent and every wisp of dissidence? No chance at all! For was this not the same Pilate who had dared to parade the icons of the emperor through the city? Was this not the same Pilate who had dressed his soldiers in civilian garb to mingle with the crowds, so as to provoke them to riot and give him a pretext to cut them down? And was not Caiaphas, whose piercing eyes and keen ears had kept him in office throughout Pilate's procurator-ship, the high priest?

With such a pair, can there be any doubt that they would have taken even fewer chances than had Herod the Tetrarch, were a charismatic of charismat-ics to appear in Jerusalem attracting crowds? Would Pontius Pilate or Caiaphas care a fig for what the man taught or preached? And if the charismatic were attracting crowds because it seemed to many that he was the Son of man, the King-Messiah about to usher in the kingdom of God, would they not pounce on him swiftly and hasten him to the cross, the ultimate Roman deterrent for keeping revolutionaries and would-be messiahs at bay? For Pontius Pilate and Caiaphas, danger to Rome lurked as much behind the visions of an Isaiah, the prophecies of an Ezekiel, the mantle of an Elijah, or the likeness of the Son of man, as behind the sheathed dagger of a Judas of Galilee.

81

A charismatic of charismatics would thus have had no chance of survival at all. To the degree that he proved himself to be such a charismatic through his healing of the sick, his casting out of demons, his raising of the dead, his arousing of hopes for the coming of God's kingdom—to that degree would he attract crowds. And if this charismatic of charismatics actually tested his faith and that of his followers by parading through Jerusalem among crowds who were chanting "the Messiah, the Son of man is among us—Hosanna in the highest," and by appearing in the Temple precincts as a champion of piety and rectitude, Caiaphas would have been provoked to decisive action, lest his failure to act be mistaken as a sign of either permissiveness or fear. With his high priestly office dangling on his detection of sparks of violence before they burst into flames, Caiaphas would lose no time in silencing so ominous a threat to law and order.

Events then would have occurred with blurring rapidity. Caiaphas would have had the charismatic of charismatics brought before his privy council, a sanhedrin of the high priest, and have charged him with undermining Roman authority by his teachings, his preachings, and his actions. For he had taught and preached that the kingdom of God was near at hand, a kingdom which, were it to come, would displace the kingdom of Rome. By creating the impression that he might be the Son of man, the King-Messiah who would usher in God's kingdom, he had, in fact, sought to reign in Caesar's stead. And by stirring up the crowds, parading as he did through Jerusalem and causing a commotion in the precincts of the Temple, he had readied the people for riotous behavior. His teachings, preachings, and actions were bound to sway the loyalties of the Jews: God disapproved of the emperor, God disapproved of the procurator, and God disapproved of the procurator-appointed high priest. The fact that the charismatic of charismatics had taught no violence, had preached no revolution, and lifted up no arms against Rome's authority would have been utterly irrelevant. The High Priest Caiaphas and the Procurator Pontius Pilate cared not a whit how or by whom the kingdom of God would be ushered in, but only that the Roman emperor and his instruments would not reign over it.

With charges such as these flung at him in the presence of Caiaphas' hand-chosen privy councillors, the fate of the charismatic would be sealed. He had undermined law and order by his words and deeds. He had sowed the seeds of mass demonstrations and contagious violence. These alone were the issues. *Neither his religious teachings nor his beliefs could have been on trial—only their potential political consequences; for the sanhedrin was the high priest's council, which had no function other than to advise the high priest on political matters.* All those who sat on this sanhedrin were committed to the doctrine of the two realms—a doctrine to which Sadducees and Pharisees and Essenes adhered. *As a body appointed and convened by a religious illegitimate, the sanhedrin of the high priest had no authority over religious matters.* Sadducees could sit beside Pharisees only as individuals concerned with preserving the compact

83

with Rome, a compact which guaranteed religious autonomy to the Jews as long as the Jews recognized Roman sovereignty. The high priest's sanhedrin thus could not have been a *bet din* (*boulé*); for the issues to be dealt with were political issues, not religious ones.

These then were the questions they would have asked themselves: Were the man's charisma and teachings attracting crowds? What were the chances that the people might go berserk and provoke the procurator into ordering out the troops? Even though the charismatic himself were a man of peace, not of violence; a visionary, not a revolutionary; a gentle and compassionate healer and teacher, not a rabble-rouser, he could release a tempest of violence. Empathy for the charismatic's plight would have been counterbalanced by empathy for the hundreds, if not thousands who might be butchered by the Roman soldiers if the crowds misheard, misunderstood, or brushed aside the pleas of the charismatic that violence was not what he had meant at all—that God, not the violence of men, would usher in his kingdom.

The outcome of such a trial would thus have been cut and dried. The high priest, as the eyes and ears of the procurator, was not a free agent. The members of the council, the sanhedrin which he convoked, were likewise not free agents. The charismatic had attracted crowds with his preachings, his wonder workings, and his charisma. As such, he was potentially dangerous. There could be few grounds for hesitancy or mitigation. *If the charismatic either claimed to be or were believed to be the Son of man,*

84

the Messiah, the King of the Jews, and if he were preaching the imminent coming of the kingdom of God, which of necessity would displace the kingdom of Rome, then the case was open and shut. There was no recourse for the high priest but to advise the procurator that the charismatic of charismatics was in contempt of the emperor and a potential source of disruption and violence, however couched his teachings might be in prophetic imagery and however much he might emphasize that the kingdom of God was to be brought in by God, not man.

The high priest and the sanhedrin would thus report to the procurator the simple facts: Here is a charismatic of charismatics who attracted crowds; who set off a disturbance in the Temple area, thronged at festival time with highly excitable pilgrims; who was acclaimed as the Messiah, the King of the Jews, as he walked through the streets of Jerusalem; and who called upon the people to prepare themselves for the coming of God's kingdom—not at some distant time in the future, as the Scribes-Pharisees taught, but at any moment—in the twinkling of an eye.

It would now be up to the procurator to make a final decision as to whether he concurred with the facts and the judgment: Was the charismatic sufficiently dangerous to be crucified as a warning to other charismatics that their religious teachings would be judged by the political consequences that might follow in their wake? *Crucifixion awaited both the revolutionary and charismatic.* Pontius

85

Pilate, a procurator notorious for his highhandedness and ruthlessness, would have made short shrift of a case like this. A rebel against Rome was a rebel against Rome, however much he cloaked his rebellion in talk of God. Such a rebel belonged on the cross—not in the hills of Galilee, or in the streets of Jerusalem, or in the precincts of the Temple. His agony, his helplessness, and his failure would discourage other charismatics from dreaming dangerous dreams. It would discourage the people at large from following dreamlike images of the Son of man, the would-be king-messiahs, the deluded weavers of a fantasy kingdom of God that would never come. For Pontius Pilate, a charismatic served up to him by his loyal and competent Caiaphas would have been a welcome opportunity for a display of Caesar's might.

But would not the teaching and preaching of the charismatic of charismatics have been so religiously provocative as to have aroused the anger of the Scribes-Pharisees? Would not the Scribes-Pharisees have been affronted by his wonder working, his casting out of demons, his cavalier disregard for the tradition of the elders, his posturing as the Son of man and the Messiah? And would they not have brought him before a *bet din (boulé)* on the charge of blasphemy or its equivalent? The answer to these questions is No! *For just as the Scribes-Pharisees adhered to the doctrine of the two realms, so too did they adhere to the doctrine of live and let live.* They did not haul Sadducees before their *bet din (boulé)*, even though the Sadducees rejected the twofold Law. They did not prohibit a Sadducean high priest from carrying out his duties in the Temple, however heretical in their sight he might have been, as long as he did not deviate from the procedures set down by the Scribes-Pharisees. They would surely challenge the claims of a charismatic: They would mock and ridicule him; pummel him with invectives; even pray for his undoing—but that was as far as they could go. Their legal jurisdiction no more extended to a charismatic than it did to Caiaphas, a Sadducee, who looked upon the oral Law as a fraud, the Scribes-Pharisees as blasphemous usurpers, and reward and punishment beyond the grave as the cruelest illusion of all.

The fate of charismatics was thus sealed by a process that began with a trial before the high priest and his sanhedrin and ended with the procurator's sentence of death by crucifixion—a process that was political throughout in its intent and purpose. His crime would have been lese majesty—proclaimed to all by the *titulus* above the cross, mocking his pretension to be the King of the Jews. The charismatic had crossed the line that separated the turf of Caesar from the turf of God. He had crossed over into that no-man's-land where every life was forfeit. He may have been naive, but his political innocence would not spare him. There was a war being waged daily in Galilee, in the streets of Jerusalem, and in the Temple courts. Thousands already had been killed, maimed, burned, and crucified. Thousands more were destined to share the same fate. The people had become ungovernable. From day to day, Pontius Pilate did not know whether he would be procurator on the morrow.

Caiaphas knew not at nightfall whether, when morning dawned, he would be high priest. One provocative act, one unguarded moment, one still small voice proclaiming the kingdom of God—and the people could go wild with a frenzy that would not calm itself until the troops had butchered Jews by the hundreds, if not thousands. With their fate precariously dangling on the edge of each decision, Pontius Pilate and Caiaphas were hardly likely to spare a charismatic of charismatics whose innocence and naiveté had allowed him to stumble over the line that separated God's turf from Caesar's.

The cross would have been the fate that awaited a charismatic of charismatics, but it would not necessarily have been his destiny. For if his disciples had come to believe that he was indeed the Son of man, and if he had bound them tightly to his person by his charisma, then there was every likelihood that their belief in him would have remained unshaken, even though they heard him gasp with his last breath, "God, why hast thou forsaken me?"—every likelihood—for at the very core of his teaching would have been his sturdy faith in the good news of the Scribes-Pharisees that souls of the righteous soar up to God the Father, where they await the day of resurrection. Nothing could have been more certain to him than this promise. Resurrection, far from being impossible, was inevitable. And if inevitable, how could it be denied by his disciples, if they saw their Teacher risen from the dead? For them, this would be the proof that he must be the Son of man, the King-Messiah.

This was a happening that would confute the Scribes-Pharisees: The charismatic of charismatics must be the Messiah, because he had risen from the dead.

Stunned, bewildered, disoriented, disbelieving the sight of their beloved Teacher crucified, would not the eyes of the faithful have seen what the eyes of the faithless could not?—that their Master, their Teacher, their Lord was as alive as he ever had been when he had preached among them! And would they not exultantly then have shouted out the good news from the rooftops, proclaimed throughout the land that the Christ had risen from the dead, that he soon would be seen coming, with the kingdom of God following in his wake? And would not their faith in what they had seen be so strong that they would have been able to withstand the challenge and mockery of the nonseers? And would it not have been so tenacious that they would even be willing to face the beasts at Ephesus with joy?

And would not, then, the difference between a charismatic of charismatics such as this man, and a charismatic such as John the Baptist, lie precisely in this: that while the charismatic's life would have ended in death, the charismatic of charismatics' death would have ended in Life?

6

Jesus, King of the Jews

We have drawn a portrait of a charismatic of charismatics whose life would have ended in Life. We have drawn it from Josephus' writings; Josephus himself did not draw it for us. It is a portrait of a charismatic who would have lived and died and been seen as resurrected. Given the time, the place, the situation, and the mind-set, this portrait is as real as life itself.

But there were those who painted portraits of a charismatic of charismatics who had actually lived—portraits which they believed expressed the very likeness of a remarkable person who had lived, died, and been seen as resurrected while Pontius Pilate was procurator and while Caiaphas was high priest. That charismatic of charismatics whose portrait they painted was Jesus the Messiah, the Son of man, the resurrected One. Yet though those portraits describe the same man, they so differ from one another as to put us at a loss to know which portrait bears the greater likeness.

We thus find ourselves in a quandary. On the one hand, we have drawn a portrait from Josephus of a charismatic of charismatics who might have lived, died, and been seen as resurrected. On the other hand, we have, in the four Gospels of Mark, Matthew, Luke, and John, portraits of Jesus drawn from real life preserved. Yet these portraits are so at variance that we cannot be certain which is most lifelike. Perhaps we can extricate ourselves from our dilemma by placing the portrait of the charismatic of charismatics that we have drawn next to the portraits of Jesus as painted in the Gospels.

Let us look first at the portrait of Jesus drawn in the Gospel of John, since that one bears the least resemblance to the one we have drawn. We find that, indeed, there is hardly any resemblance at all. John's portrait of Jesus is one we could not have imagined from the writings of Josephus. It is a portrait that presupposes a different time, a different space, and a different mind-set. It is a portrait appropriate for a historical setting where the Christian communities are made up entirely of Gentiles and are spread throughout the cities of the Roman world. These Christians are far more interested in the Son of God, whose destiny was the cross and resurrection, than in the Son of man, who had preached the coming of God's kingdom to redeem the household of Israel. John's Gospel sees Jesus almost exclusively in the light of the resurrection, rather than in the light of history. What Jesus actually said and did while he was alive was significant, in John's view, only to the degree that it reflected or illuminated Christ's divine (not human) destiny. For John, Jesus is the divine

91

light whose humanity refracts his divinity. He is no mere mortal, a simple charismatic of charismatics whose humanity stirs the hearts and souls of those he touches and whose teaching arouses within them the hope for the coming of God's kingdom.

This divine role is evident the moment we open the Gospel of John. The Evangelist does not begin with a prophetic proclamation, as does Mark; or with a genealogy, as does Matthew; or with an assurance that his Gospel can be relied upon as accurately portraying Jesus' words and deeds, as does Luke. Instead, John begins with an outright declaration that God and the Logos, the Word of God, are one and the same and that they are the source of light and life (1:1-4). John the Baptist, according to the Evangelist, came not to announce that someone greater than he was to be the Redeemer, but to bear witness to the divine Light which was about to come into the world (1:19ff). Though John portrays the Christ as the divine Light, he is not recognized as such by the Jews to whom he first appears. He is, however, recognized as the divine Light by the Gentiles (1:11-12).

Jesus' own people were thus blind to the divine Light. They were so blind that they hounded him and conspired with the authorities to have him crucified. The Gentiles, not the Jews, are thus the true seed of Abraham. Jesus' kinsmen in the flesh had shown themselves to be no kinsmen in the Spirit. The Gentiles alone proved worthy of being the people of God. The Gospel of John thus elevates Jesus out of his historical setting onto a timeless plane. Whereas the Synoptic Gospels are enigmatic as to the purpose of Jesus' ultimate fate, the Gospel of John is certain that he came to be crucified and to be resurrected.

From the very beginning of the Gospel of John, Christ's earthly sojourn is a trajectory from Light to Light, from Life to Life, and from Father to Father. The Christ passes through this world in a body of flesh and blood, only in order that his divinity may shine forth—first through his life, then through his "death" and resurrection. All who saw the Light shining through his life and were enlightened by it were destined to enjoy eternal life. The crucifixion was thus inexorable and necessary. It was something Jesus anticipated and welcomed. It was an event which revealed the blindness of the Jews who sought his crucifixion; an event which exposed their malevolence; an event which demonstrated that they were unworthy of remaining the people of God—an unworthiness they revealed when they refused to see Jesus risen from the dead. By contrast, the Gentiles demonstrated their worthiness to replace the Jews as the people of God when they saw Jesus risen from the dead and when they believed what they saw.

It is not surprising, therefore, that when we read the Gospel of John, we see a Jesus above time, above place, above constraining frameworks. John sets Jesus off from the Jews as though Jesus himself had been a Gentile. He seems unaware that not all Jews were Pharisees and overlooks Jesus' controversies with the Pharisees regarding the binding character of the Traditions of the Elders. Likewise, John's failure to refer to the Scribes, mentioning only the

93

Pharisees, illuminates how little John seems to know or care about the historical setting in which Jesus preached. So, too, John's use of the term *Passover* to refer to the entire festival is at odds with the Synoptics' distinction between Passover, which refers only to the first day of the festival, and Feast of Unleavened Bread, which in Jesus' day was the designation for the remaining days of the festival. John's portrait of Jesus thus bears little resemblance to our portrait drawn from Josephus—that of a charismatic of charismatics emerging out of the matrix of time, structure, process, and causality.

Not so with the Synoptic Gospels. The portraits of Jesus found in the Gospels of Mark, Matthew, and Luke portray a Jesus who, however much he may have been "out of this world," was part and parcel of it as well. He is pictured as a prophetlike figure, a charismatic of charismatics, the Son of man who enjoys a special relationship to God the Father. In Mark, we are told that there were some people who believed that Jesus was John the Baptist resurrected, and hence endowed with miraculous powers; there were others who believed him to be Elijah; there were still others who believed that he was a prophet like the prophets of old—all images evoking charismatics whom God had endowed with supernatural powers (6:14-16). And even when Jesus is transfigured, he is pictured as being with Elijah and Moses as one who, like them, had a special relationship with God (Matthew 17:3; Mark 9:4; Luke 9:30). Here Jesus is humanized, personalized, and historicized. Jesus becomes credible because he

94

is reminiscent of an Elijah and a Moses. He is not a divine being with no biblical prototype.

The portraits in the Synoptic Gospels, with all their differences in shading and nuance, stand out in sharp contrast to John's portrait of Jesus. There are clearly discernible features which bear a striking resemblance to the charismatic of charismatics whom we have drawn from Josephus. For the words and deeds of our projected charismatic of charismatics, like those of Jesus, would have evoked images of John the Baptist, Elijah, Moses, and the prophets of old in the minds of those who listened to Jesus and observed his wonder working powers. So too, Jesus' journey from life to Life as traced in the Synoptic Gospels is the very trajectory which our projected charismatic of charismatics would have taken—the path of a person of flesh and blood, in whom the Spirit of God dwelled and who became thereby worthy of resurrection.

This human life of Jesus as delineated in the Synoptic Gospels sets him firmly in the historical matrix of the times. John the Baptist, a real charismatic, is held up as a precursor and a prototype. He is the same good man in the Synoptics as in Josephus. He is the voice crying in the wilderness, preaching a baptism of repentance and proclaiming the coming of God's kingdom—a kingdom not to be ushered in by him, but by one who is to come after him, one more blessed and more worthy than he. Whereas John baptized with water, he who is to come will baptize with the Holy Spirit (Mark 1:2-4, 7-8; cf. Matthew 3:2, 11-12; Luke 3:4-6, 15-18). Mark and the other Synoptic Gospel writers are telling their readers that while John the Baptist was only a charismatic, Jesus was a charismatic of charismatics.

As such, Jesus trudges a road of his own making. Though frequenting the synagogue, he does not acknowledge any limitations on his teachings: He speaks out with a *singular* authority, an authority that arouses astonishment because it is so unlike the authority of the Scribes-Pharisees, which was collective, not individual. As the Son of man, Jesus does not hesitate to pronounce God's forgiveness of the sins of a paralytic, even though this divinelike act arouses the Scribes, who insist that God alone has the power to forgive sins. They charge Jesus with blasphemy, to which Jesus replies that, as the Son of man, he does have that authority (Matthew 9:1-8; Mark 2:1-12; Luke 5:17-26).

Jesus is no less defiant when he eats with sinners and tax collectors, even though the Scribes-Pharisees disapprove. When Jesus explains that he has come to call only sinners, not the righteous, they become even more infuriated, since his words bespeak a rejection of their authority (Matthew 9:9-13; Mark 2:13-17; Luke 5:27-32). Nor can the Scribes-Pharisees submit to Jesus' right to take the Law into his own hands when he allows his disciples to pluck ears of grain on the sabbath (Matthew 12:1-8; Mark 2:23-28; Luke 6:1-5); or when he shrugs off their eating with unwashed hands (Matthew 15:1-20; Mark 7:1-23); or when he himself heals a man's withered arm on the sabbath (Matthew 12:9-14; Mark 3:1-6; Luke 6:6-11). Brushing aside the Traditions of the Elders as man-made, not

God-made, he denounces his accusers as hypocrites (Mark 7:8-13; cf. Matthew 15:3-9).

Confronted with such behavior, the Scribes-Pharisees were at a loss as to what manner of man this was who healed the sick and spoke so assuredly of the kingdom of God which was about to come. Was he a teacher? (Mark 9:38). Was he a prophet, like one of the prophets of old? Elijah? Or even Moses, perhaps? Was he John, resurrected from the dead? (Matthew 14:1-2; Mark 6:14-16; Luke 9:7-9). Was he the Son of man? Was he the Messiah who would restore the kingdom of father David? (Mark 11:9-10; cf. Matthew 21:9; Luke 12:38). And what of his impressive powers and charisma—were they of God, or were they of Beelzebul, the Prince of Demons? (Matthew 12:22-24; Mark 3:19-22; Luke 11:14-16).

Sitting in Moses' seat, the Pharisees were forced to take a stand. Jesus, they concluded, was no simple replica of John the Baptist. He was a messianic pretender and, as such, must be exposed as a fraud. This the Scribes-Pharisees tried to do by using their authority to undermine his claims. If Jesus exorcised demons, then he must be Beelzebul's instrument (Matthew 12:24; Mark 3:22; Luke 11:15). If he healed on the sabbath day, he must be a violator of the Law (Matthew 12:10; Mark 3:2; Luke 6:7). If he allowed his disciples to eat with unwashed hands (Matthew 15:2; Mark 7:5) or to pluck ears of grain on the sabbath (Matthew 12:2; Mark 2:24; Luke 6:2), he was mocking the Traditions of the Elders. If he forgave sins, he was a blasphemer (Matthew 9:2-3; Mark 2:5-7; Luke 5:20-21). If he seemed to be a prophet, where were his signs? (Matthew 12:38). If he were the Anointed, where was Elijah? (Matthew 17:10; Mark 9:11). If he were the Messiah, son of David, where was his genealogy? (Matthew 22:41-42; Mark 12:35; Luke 20:41). If he preached that the kingdom of God was coming, should the tribute to Caesar be paid, or not? (Matthew 22:17; Mark 12:14; Luke 20:22).

It is one thing, however, to *try* to expose Jesus as a fraud; it is quite another to succeed. Jesus proves to be nimble-minded. He returns barb for barb. Beelzebul, the Prince of Demons, would scarcely destroy his own house (Matthew 12:25-26; Mark 3:23-26; Luke 11:17-18). The Son of man, he claims with a proof text to hand, need not be a descendant of David (Matthew 22:41-45; Mark 12:36-37; Luke 20:42-44). As for the payment of tribute, he, *echoing the Scribes-Pharisees*, insists that one must render unto Caesar what is Caesar's and unto God what is God's (Matthew 22:21; Mark 12:17; Luke 20:25).

The Scribes-Pharisees again and again find themselves mystified. On occasion, Jesus appears to be an exemplary teacher, adroitly and deftly countering the Sadducees who poke fun at the belief in resurrection (Matthew 22:23-33; Mark 12:18-27; Luke 20:27-40). And he draws the approval of a Scribe-Pharisee by affirming that "Hear, O Israel: The Lord our God, the Lord is one; and you shall love the Lord your God with all your heart, and with all your soul, and with all your mind, and with all your strength," is the heart of the Law, while loving one's neighbor as oneself runs a close second (Mark 12:28-34; cf. Matthew 22:34-40; Luke 10:25-28).

The Scribes-Pharisees thus had no easy time in challenging Jesus. He seemed at times to be one of them, but again, he seemed not to be one of them at all. He adhered to the core teachings of the Scribes-Pharisees, yet flaunted their authority by claiming a special relationship to God and by making light of the Traditions of the Elders. Thus when Jesus sought to compare his authority to that of John the Baptist, the Scribes-Pharisees, though left speechless, would have none of it (Mark 11:27-33). John may indeed have been a charismatic like Jesus, but he had kept his charisma within acceptable bounds. John had called for repentance, as did the Scribes-Pharisees—only more so. He had called for piety, as did the Scribes-Pharisees—only more so. He had called for justice, as did the Scribes-Pharisees—only more so. John's call to baptism as a sign of the inner purification of the soul was a call the Scribes-Pharisees could applaud. Though John had proclaimed that the kingdom of God was at hand, he had not embarrassed the Scribes-Pharisees as had Jesus, with his allusions to being the Son of man or the King-Messiah.

Yet John's benign teachings had not spared him a tragic fate. His eloquence had attracted crowds, and crowds were dangerous. The political authorities took no chances. They had put him to death, though Josephus looked upon John as a good and righteous man. Jesus' teachings would thus be even more threatening. They were far more disruptive than any advanced by John. For Jesus, unlike John, had provoked the Scribes-Pharisees by flaunting his special relationship to God and by persisting in

99

his ways: His healings continued; his exorcisms continued; his sitting with sinners continued; his preaching of the coming kingdom of God continued. And crowds gathered round him to hear, to see, to hope; and they struck fear in the heart of Caiaphas.

The more demons Jesus exorcised, the more mustard seeds he spread abroad, the more crowds he drew, the more irresistible his claims to be the Son of man, the King-Messiah, the redeemer of Israel, the more the authorities feared an incident in the crowded streets of Jerusalem. They especially feared a demonstration on the Temple mount, as tens of thousands of Jews crowded into Jerusalem—perhaps a more violent demonstration than that described in the Gospels when Jesus overthrew the tables of the moneychangers and cried out that the Temple had become a den of robbers. The crowds were feared no less when they shouted in the streets, "Hosanna! Blessed is he who comes in the name of the Lord! Blessed is the kingdom of our father David that is coming! Hosanna in the highest!" (Mark 11:9-10).

It would make no difference to the political authorities whether such incidents were sparked by religious zeal or by political expectations; or whether these incidents were spontaneous or orchestrated outbursts. *Indeed, it mattered not who said what, or what sparked who, or who sparked what, or what the political motivation of the sparker happened to be. Even if Jesus had pleaded for measured calm by calling out, "This is not what I meant at all, not at all," it would have made no difference to the authorities.* What mattered were the consequences for high priest and procurator if the crowds had gone wild, shouting "The kingdom of God is at hand, and Jesus is our King." The coming of God's kingdom would, in fact, have been even more frightening to Pontius Pilate and Caiaphas than a mere human kingdom, since God's kingdom could be blocked by no earthly power, however exalted and mighty.

The Synoptic Gospels portray Caiaphas and Pontius Pilate as doing exactly what we would have expected them to do, knowing as we do the tragic fate of John the Baptist. We are not surprised, therefore, to learn that Caiaphas moved against Jesus as quietly as he could, lest angry crowds gather; had him brought, as we would have expected, before the high priest's sanhedrin of privy councillors, hand-picked for their loyalty to the doctrine of two realms and for their sense of concern for a savage Roman response to any riotous behavior of the crowds, irrespective of its source (Matthew 26:3-5, 57-68).

The followers of Jesus thus told it as it had actually happened. *Jesus was brought before the only body that had jurisdiction over those who were charged with breaking or endangering the peace: the high priest's sanhedrin, convoked by him and presided over by him. Despite the hostility they may have harbored for the Scribes-Pharisees, the disciples of Jesus did not report that Jesus had been brought before a bet din (boulé), presided over by a teacher of the twofold Law, to be charged with a violation of God's Law. They did not so report because in Jesus' day, all Jews living in Judea and Galilee knew that a charismatic would never be*

101

brought before a religious body to stand trial for his life, however deviant his religious teachings.

The Synoptic Gospels' accounts are thus historically credible, since they exonerate the *bet din (boulé)* from any role in the trial and crucifixion of Jesus. They bear true witness to the imperial system and its jurisdiction over political issues; to the doctrine of the two realms espoused by the Scribes-Pharisees with respect to the political and religious realms; and to the doctrine of live and let live with respect to divergent forms of Judaism.

The Gospels likewise confirm our expectations when they tell us that Jesus was charged with the crime of being the Son of man, the Messiah, the King of the Jews. *For the issue was not a religious issue, even though these images were grounded in the Hebrew Scriptures.* The prophets had envisioned an end of days when all pain and suffering and anguish—even death itself—would be stilled. Isaiah had visualized a King-Messiah, sprung from the stump of Jesse, who would reign in glory. Ezekiel had been addressed by God as the Son of man.

And here lies the tragedy of it all: These images rooted in Scriptures did indeed have political implications. God's kingdom in was Rome's kingdom out! There was no way Jesus' preaching of God's kingdom could be disentangled from politics. *The high priest, the high priest's sanhedrin, and the procurator—all were bound to look upon Jesus' teachings as politically dangerous, however free they were of overt political intent.* Jesus' preaching of the coming of God's kingdom was treasonous in their eyes, as long as that kingdom had no place

102

for the Roman emperor, his procurator, and his procurator-appointed high priest. Only if Jesus were in truth the Son of man and the King-Messiah could the prophetic promise of a messianic age be acknowledged as having been fulfilled in him. But this was dependent on his actually bringing in the kingdom despite all human efforts to block it. In a word, Jesus would need to prove his claim by living, not by dying.

The Synoptic Gospels thus confirm that Jesus suffered the fate which would have befallen the charismatic of charismatics we have drawn from Josephus. For the Gospels tell us that Jesus was brought before Caiaphas, an appointee of the procurator, and before the high priest's sanhedrin—not before a *bet din (boulé)* of the Scribes-Pharisees—and charged with having claimed to be the Messiah, the King of the Jews. But though the Gospels clearly testify that Jesus was tried by a political body, the followers of Jesus may have believed that he had been tried on religious grounds. *For in their eyes, Jesus was the Son of man, God's Anointed*—a divinely, not a humanly crowned King. He was necessarily a fulfillment of God's promise. He was thus, ipso facto, a religious, not a political figure.

The high priest and his sanhedrin, however, had no such belief. For them, Jesus was deluded, and his followers were deluded. He was just another would-be messiah whose naive illusions could spark an uprising. It is not surprising, therefore, that Jesus' disciples, who believed him to be the Christ, would attribute religious motives to the high priest and his sanhedrin, since for the disciples, Jesus was exclusively a religious instrument of God, not a political figure. No wonder, then, that the Gospels blur the distinction between the political and the religious motivations, of which the high priest and his sanhedrin were always conscious.

This same blurring envelopes Pontius Pilate. Here, too, the Gospels fulfill our expectations. Jesus, like any charismatic, would have been brought before the procurator, once the high priest and his sanhedrin were convinced that he was a threat to law and order. The procurator, for his part, would ask only one question: Are you the King of the Jews? And he would not be diverted by some Delphic answer such as, "You have said so" (Matthew 27:11; Mark 15:2; Luke 23:3). For Pontius Pilate, the judgment of his trusted high priest, Caiaphas, would have been enough.

But Pontius Pilate, as we know from Josephus, had his own political agendas. As one who was given to provoking Jews with wily strategems, Pilate was not beyond using a politically naive charismatic, one who claimed to be their King, to entrap the Jews. By giving the crowds a choice between the release of a revolutionary* such as Barabbas, who made no claim to being King of the Jews, and a charismatic who did make such a claim, Pilate was, in effect, compelling the crowd to choose the revolutionary. They would fear to choose the other, lest Pilate loose his soldiery on them for acknowledging a king other than Caesar (Matthew 27:15-23; Mark 15:6-15; Luke 23:18-25).

*Josephus invariably uses *lestos* to mean *revolutionary*, not *robber*.

Pontius Pilate's strategy, however, could hardly have been discerned by the politically naive followers of Jesus. All they could see and comprehend was that the crowds, egged on by the priests, were calling for Barabbas. Little wonder that *their* anger would be directed against the other Jews, rather than against Pontius Pilate, who was taunting the crowd to name Jesus as their king. When we read of this incident in the light of our knowledge of Pilate's provocative tricks, we are struck by its ring of historical truth.

The Gospels have no surprises for us, either, in their account of the crucifixion or in their attestation of Jesus' resurrection. After all, the *titulus* above the cross spelled out precisely why Jesus was crucified: He was accused of having proclaimed himself King of the Jews (Matthew 27:37; Mark 15:26; Luke 23:38). *Having been found guilty of treason, was not Jesus fated for crucifixion, the punishment designed especially for those who dared to challenge the authority of Rome?* The *titulus* preserved in the Gospels thus leaves us in no doubt as to *why* Jesus was crucified, and *by whom*. And the fact that on either side of him was a revolutionary suffering the same fate evokes for us Rome's determination to eradicate anyone who challenged its rule, whether violent revolutionary or charismatic visionary.

Jesus' last words as reported in the Gospels (Mark 15:34) likewise come to us as no surprise. These are words which might very well have sprung to the lips of a charismatic when confronted with the implications of his approaching death. Sharing the belief held by all Jews that the Messiah would bring in

105

the kingdom of God during his time on earth, a charismatic would realize, when death was imminent, that his messianic hopes had been dashed. Every would-be messiah knew that there was only one test for his claims: Had he, or had he not brought in the kingdom of God in his lifetime? His own demise, whether by the sword or by the cross, would bring an end to his messianic pretensions. When, therefore, a charismatic found himself at death's door, the frightening thought that God had misled him was bound to well up within him. Twisted with pain beyond endurance, his tragic plight would evoke the psalmist's cry, so expressive of his own feelings of wretched wonder: "My God, my God, why hast thou forsaken me?"

Christians understandably interpret the meaning of this verse differently. For Christians, the Gospels are the repository of the living Christ, fused with a Jesus who lived, preached, healed the sick, exorcised demons, sat with sinners, turned the other cheek, clashed with the Pharisees, and underwent a trial, a condemnation, and a crucifixion prior to being seen risen from the dead by his disciples. Few indeed are the Christians who would deny the historical value of the Gospel accounts, even though they may point out that the historical Jesus is beyond our direct knowledge. However Christians might evaluate the historicity of Jesus, all would agree that the historical Jesus is but a limited aspect of Jesus Christ's importance for them. Christianity is not about the man, though man he was as well, but about the Jesus who is the Christ because he rose from the dead. It was only because Jesus was the Christ and not just Jesus, a charismatic of charismatics, that he became the focus of the Gospels. As the risen Christ, Jesus' historical destiny lies in his elevation above history.

The Gospel writers thus tell us of this Jesus Christ who must have been aware that he would rise from the dead, even while he was still alive. Indeed, he had made known to his disciples, however veiled the allusions, that he would rise from the dead— allusions that his disciples may not have understood at the time. When, therefore, he cried out from the cross, "My God, my God, why hast thou forsaken me?" the Gospel writers, viewing Jesus' life and crucifixion in light of the resurrection which had already occurred for them, could not possibly take Jesus' cry literally. Jesus, as the Christ of the Evangelists, must surely have known that God had not forsaken him.

The non-Christian historian has no means for weighing and measuring the facts as attested to by faith. When, therefore, he deduces a charismatic of charismatics from the writings of Josephus, he is limited in his deductions—deductions about the way this charismatic of charismatics would have responded to his imminent death—by his knowledge of what was anticipated from a Messiah by the Jews of Jesus' day. The historian cannot know of a messianic belief which requires a death followed by a resurrection to prove one's messianic claims, until such a belief emerges for the first time in the history

107

of the messianic idea. Even the disciples of Jesus had to wait three days following his crucifixion before they witnessed the risen Jesus. The historian can, perhaps, anticipate a quantum leap into novelty, but he cannot know what this novelty will actually consist of until the leap has occurred. Lacking this foreknowledge, the historian has no choice other than to read these words of Jesus on the cross as among the most pathetic ever uttered in the annals of history.

We thus face an unbridgeable chasm—a chasm separating the charismatic of charismatics drawn by a non-Christian historian from the writings of Josephus, and the Jesus who proved himself to be the Christ through his resurrection—a resurrection attested to by his disciples, but neither attested to nor believed by any known Scribe-Pharisee other than Paul.

This chasm that separates the historical Jesus from Jesus the risen Christ is wide and deep. It cannot be bridged by the historian, because he has no criteria by which the testimony of faith can be weighed and measured. It is a chasm that the historian should not cross, because he cannot cross. When, therefore, he points out that within the Synoptic Gospels that were written to record the teachings, the preachings, the wondrous acts, and the life odyssey of Jesus the risen Christ, he can also find a Jesus who resembles the portrait of the charismatic of charismatics drawn from Josephus, the historian is thereby neither displacing nor passing judgment on the portraits found in the Gospels. For Christians, the Gospel portraits of the Christ are historically true since they were drawn not simply from life, but from Life. As such, they are portraits in which the this-worldly features of Jesus the charismatic are subordinated to the otherworldly features of Jesus the Christ who rose from the dead.

As a non-Christian historian, I have merely attempted to compare the this-worldly features found within the Synoptic Gospels with those features that resemble the portrait of a charismatic of charismatics drawn from Josephus. Such a comparison reveals that though the Gospel writers are drawing portraits of Jesus the risen Christ, they have included within those portraits a picture of a historical Jesus. The Gospels thus turn out to be precious sources for our knowledge both of the historical Jesus and of Jesus the risen Christ.

Even the witnessing of Jesus risen from the dead, with the new meaning of the Messiah to which it gave birth, lay deep though dormant in the womb of Pharisaism. After all, the Scribes-Pharisees daily had taught that every righteous individual would some day be rewarded by being raised from the dead. Resurrection was not only possible, but inevitable. This was the very belief the Gospels tell us was preached during his lifetime by Jesus himself—the belief that even gained him much praise from a Scribe who was so pleased with Jesus' artful use of a proof text from Scripture to confute the Sadducees, who did not believe in resurrection. The historical Jesus had seeded in the minds of his disciples the absolute certainty that resurrection would someday occur. When, therefore, these disciples saw their

Master and Teacher dead on the cross, when their faith in his claims were being so violently assaulted by the seeming fact of his death, their eyes were already open to believe what they were to see only three days later: Jesus fully alive as the Christ. Since the fact of resurrection was for them, as for the Scribes-Pharisees, not only possible but inevitable, they did not brush aside what they saw as a fantasy, an illusion, or a wish fulfillment. Rather, they saw in the risen Christ the absolute proof that Jesus must be the Messiah—a proof that was there for all except those blinded by faithlessness to see.

We thus have found within the Gospels a historical Jesus, however subordinated he may be to Jesus the risen Christ. That historical Jesus is the Jesus whose features are identical with those of the charismatic of charismatics drawn from Josephus. In our reconstruction, we do not draw upon those features that are not identical, though we make no claim that there are not other such features as well. Bound only by the portrait of the charismatic of charismatics we have drawn from Josephus, we have freely searched these features out in all the Gospels, irrespective of the time they were written and their differing perspectives.

And that historical Jesus who peers forth in the Gospel stories is the same Jesus who followed John the Baptist; who reached lovingly to the poor and the wretched; who healed the sick, exorcised demons, broke bread with sinners, stood his ground against the Scribes-Pharisees, spoke in parables, preached an ethic and a morality that seemed to defy human nature; who proclaimed that the kingdom of God was at hand and that the time for making oneself ready was short; who intimated that he might indeed be the Son of man, the Messiah whom God had selected to usher in his kingdom and had invested with an authority that freed him from the strictures of the Scribes-Pharisees; who cried out against all those who blocked the way for God's kingdom and turned over the tables of the moneychangers in the Temple in a fit of religious zeal; who attracted crowds with the eloquence of his teaching and preaching and stirred up the fears of the high priest that these crowds might get out of hand; who was arrested by orders of the high priest and was tried by the high priest's sanhedrin on the political implications of his nonviolent, nonpolitical teaching and preaching; who was brought before Pontius Pilate, the only authority with the power to determine his ultimate fate; who died an agonizing death on the cross, positioned between two revolutionaries, with the words, "My God, my God, why hast thou forsaken me?" on his lips; who was seen risen from the dead by his faithful disciples who had heard him speak time and time again of the resurrection that awaited all those who heeded God's Word; and who, once risen, was proclaimed to be the Christ who would soon be bringing the kingdom of God.

This, we can suggest, is the historical Jesus that is to be found in the Gospels, and it is one and the same as the charismatic of charismatics we have deduced from Josephus. Not simply a charismatic, but a charismatic of charismatics—one of those rare spirits who burst into this world at infrequent intervals to confront ordinary humans and mere charismatics with a life that is out of this world, and a love that is out of this world, and a hope that is out of this world. And because such a one is out of this world, there are few who can emulate his life or his Life. The world closes in and spreads a veil of human frailties over him, leaving, even in the records of his life, only shadows of that life in this world. For had Jesus not been a spirit so rare when he walked among men, would his life not have ended with death, rather than with Life?

7

What Crucified Jesus?

Throughout the centuries, Jews and Christians have struggled with the Gospel legacy. As the only record of Jesus' life, ministry, trial, crucifixion, and attested resurrection, it has been cherished by believing Christians as the story of Moses in the Pentateuch has been cherished by believing Jews. Just as Jesus is reported in the Gospel of Matthew (5:17-18) to have told his followers that he had come not to abolish the Law, but to fulfill it, so Christian ministers have preached to their flocks that not one iota, not one dot of the Gospel story will pass away until all that is taught within it is accomplished. So trustworthy indeed was the record for believing Christians that they could offer no more powerful attestation to the veracity of any statement than to affirm it as "gospel" truth.

However, what was gospel truth for Christians was gospel untruth for Jews. Until very recent times, all Jews regarded the Gospels as false revelation and looked upon Jesus as a false messiah. For Jews, the

Gospels seemed to be the source of their tragic experience with Christians, not only throughout the Middle Ages but into modern times as well. Jews found in the Gospels the source of the harassments, the humiliations, the pogroms, and the expulsions which have plagued them to this day, the day of the Holocaust. Indeed, there are many Jews who are convinced that anti-Semitism will never pass away until every jot and tittle of the Gospel stories is erased. As long as Christians read in the Gospels of Jesus' denunciation of the Scribes-Pharisees as hypocrites, whitewashed tombs, vipers, and sons of hell (Matthew 23:13-33); as long as Christians read as gospel truth the cry "Crucify him," shouted by the Jews before Pilate (Mark 15:13; cf. Matthew 27:22, Luke 23:21, John 19:6), or the insistence of the Jews that Pilate should crucify Jesus because "We have a law, and by that law he ought to die, because he has made himself Son of God" (John 19:7), anti-Semitism is the cross that Jews living among Christians will be forced to bear.

Some salvation for Jews seemed to be at hand with the spread of critical biblical scholarship in the nineteenth and twentieth centuries. Non-Jewish scholars, many of them Christians, subjected the Gospel accounts to scrutiny and concluded that however much truth they might contain, the Gospel stories fall far short of being the gospel truth. Although some of those non-Jewish scholars may have been anti-Semitic, and most of them looked upon Christianity as a higher stage of religion than Judaism, they nonetheless opened the sluice gates for challenge of the Gospels. Indeed, some went so

114

far as to raise the question as to whether a Jesus had actually lived. If the Gospels then were not gospel truth, the harsh anti-Jewish passages in the New Testament could be ascribed to the long, tortuous process by which the earliest traditions about Jesus were amplified, expanded, even negated by the changing needs of the Christian communities as they spread into the Gentile world. Jesus' hostility toward Jews that emanates from the Gospels could be mitigated by transferring that hostility from Jesus to the Gospel writers, writers who had attributed to the historical Jesus the hostile feelings of a later age.

Yet there are empirical facts that cannot be dissolved. Only were we to agree with those few scholars who question whether there was a Jesus, could we dodge the facts that Jesus was tried, crucified, and seen by his followers as resurrected during the procuratorship of Pontius Pilate and the high priesthood of Caiaphas. And if these bare facts are true, then the question of responsibility is certain to be raised again and again. For Jesus was no ordinary man, and his crucifixion and attested resurrection were no ordinary events. His life, his trial, his crucifixion, and the faith in his resurrection launched a religion of enormous profundity and power. For his followers, his life, trial, crucifixion, and rising from the dead were facts before which all other facts must bow. And of all these facts *for faith*, the fact of his resurrection is the fact nonpareil, for without that belief, however visualized, there would have been no Christianity. Had Jesus' life ended with death, his fate would have been no different from that of John the Baptist—no matter how many withered arms he had healed, how many demons he had exorcised, or how many wretched he had comforted. It was only because his life ended in Life that Christianity was endowed with life. But without the claim that he was the Son of man, the King-Messiah, and without the crucifixion that followed from that claim, there could have been no resurrection. So whatever the findings of critical scholarship, a triad of facts—trial, crucifixion, attested resurrection—undergird Christianity.

The collision between Jews and Christians over the facts that revolve around Jesus as the Messiah, and around Jesus' resurrection, is a collision that should no longer be necessary. Although the wish to spread the good news about Jesus and the good news about Judaism is not only understandable but desirable, the likelihood that Jews will ever accept the resurrection as a fact, or that believing Christians will ever be convinced that the resurrection did not occur, is remote indeed. As faith communities, Judaism and Christianity follow paths that do not intersect.

But when it comes to the trial and crucifixion, collision between Jews and Christians would seem to be inevitable. The Gospels have drawn up a bill of indictment, an indictment that is bound to provoke the question, Who Crucified Jesus? And once the question is thus phrased, we instinctively focus on the persons responsible. And those persons are seen to be, with the exception of Pontius Pilate, Jews. But *should our focus shift from casting blame on persons to casting blame on the time, the place, and the situation, we may be able to view the issue in a new light.* Perhaps it was not *who* one was, but *what* one was, that is the crux. *For it emerges with great clarity, both from Josephus and from the Gospels, that the culprit is not the Jews, but the Roman imperial system.* It was the Roman emperor who appointed the procurator; it was the procurator who appointed the high priest; and it was the high priest who convoked his privy council. It was the Roman imperial system which exacted harsh tribute. It was the actions of Roman procurators which drove the people wild and stirred Judea with convulsive violence. And it was the Roman imperial system which bred revolutionaries and seeded charismatics.

It was the Roman imperial system that was at fault, not the system of Judaism. The Sadducees, Scribes-Pharisees, and Essenes pushed no one to violent revolt, sowed no soil to breed charismatics. Neither biblical writ nor oral Law allowed for the high priest to be elevated into or tossed out of the high priestly office at the whim of puppet king or arrogant procurator. Nor was there to be found in either the written or oral Law any provision for the high priest to convoke a sanhedrin for any purpose whatsoever. So far removed in that day were the Sadducees, Scribes-Pharisees, and Essenes from punitive actions against those who might preach aberrant ideas, that the Scribes-Pharisees allowed Sadducean high priests to enter the Holy of Holies on the Day of Atonement, provided they followed Pharisaic procedures. And they allowed Sadducees to preach their heretical views, provided they did not act them out publicly.

117

And insofar as the *bet din* (*boulé*) of the Pharisees was concerned, it exercised jurisdiction only over those who freely chose to follow the teachings of the Scribes-Pharisees; over the conduct of public worship; and over the liturgical calendar. Not only was the *bet din* a *boulé* and not a sanhedrin, but it was presided over by a nasi, not the high priest, and it consisted exclusively of teachers of the twofold Law. Had there been no Roman imperial system, Jesus would have faced the buffetings of strong words, the batterings of skillfully aimed proof texts, and the ridicule of both Sadducees and Scribes-Pharisees, but he would have stood no trial, been affixed to no cross.

And what is striking is that the Gospels confirm that no institution of Judaism had anything to do with the trial and crucifixion of Jesus. We find in the Gospels that the high priest was appointed in violation of both the onefold and the twofold Law; that the high priest's sanhedrin convoked by him had no warrant from either the onefold or the twofold Law; that the procurator was appointed by Rome, with no sanction from either the onefold or the twofold Law; and that the penalty of crucifixion was nowhere provided for in either the onefold or the twofold Law. One searches in the Gospels for the *bet din* (*boulé*) of the Scribes-Pharisees; for the nasi who presided over it; for the procedures spelled out by either the written or the oral Law; or the specific written or oral law that Jesus had violated—but all in vain.

What we do find is that Joseph of Arimathea, a member of the *boulé*—*not* the sanhedrin—seeks to give Jesus a Jewish burial (Mark 15:43; cf. Luke 23:50); that the Nasi Gamaliel urges the sanhedrin to let Peter and his associates go free (Acts 5:34 ff.); that Paul disrupts a sanhedrin when the Pharisees support his belief in resurrection (Acts 23:6-10); and that Jesus is seen risen from the dead, as the core teaching of the Scribes-Pharisees allowed.

It is true that the Gospels portray the Scribes-Pharisees as challenging Jesus' claims, and it is true that the Scribes-Pharisees are pictured as cooperating with the authorities, but that is a far cry from having religious jurisdiction. The Scribes-Pharisees confronted the Sadducees with no less angry, harsh, even vituperative words—but words only. And as for the Scribes-Pharisees' cooperation with the authorities, such cooperation was not a result of concern over the religious consequences, but the tragic *political* consequences that could befall the entire Jewish people.

And those political consequences could be devastating indeed. Thousands of Jews had lost their lives only a few years before in the aftermath of the pulling down of the golden eagle. Uncounted others had been slain in bloody encounters between religiously motivated procurators and puppet kings. Rulers in Jesus' day knew that prophetic visions were not to be trifled with, just as they had known it in the days of Jeremiah. Frightened by the crowds drawn to Jesus' charisma, and absolutely certain themselves that Jesus was not the Messiah and that the kingdom of God was not at hand, some Scribes-Pharisees may have voiced their concern for the tragic consequences that might follow, should

119

the crowds get out of hand and go on a rampage. They reasoned, even as Herod the Tetrarch had reasoned, that it was risky to take chances when the stakes were so high. There may have been a sharing of these concerns—concerns that did not arise from the religious content of Jesus' teachings, but from their political implications for the authorities. The Scribes-Pharisees, after all, were committed to both the doctrine of live and let live in the religious sphere and the doctrine of the two realms in the political sphere.

It is this doctrine of render to Caesar the things that are Caesar's, and to God the things that are God's that was the gut issue. It was a doctrine that the Scribes-Pharisees, the Sadducees, and the Essenes all subscribed to because it held out the hope of the preservation of the people of Israel as a people of God. The essence of that designation was the covenant that had been made with God—not with the Roman emperor. And that covenant called for obedience to God's revealed Law: the written Law, for the Sadducees; the written and the oral Law, for the Scribes-Pharisees; the written Law and other holy writings, for the Essenes. As long as that covenant could be kept, the issue of political sovereignty was irrelevant. After all, had not the Aaronide priests, for more than two centuries, tended the altar and preserved the covenant under the imperial sway—first of the Persians, then of Alexander, then of the Ptolemies? If the preservation of God's covenant required subservience to Roman rule, the payment of tribute to Rome, or helpless inaction as Roman legions repressed unruly crowds, then this was but a small price to pay for spiritual survival. It was not by might or by power, but by the Spirit, that the people of God were to be sustained.

Render to Caesar the things that are Caesar's, and to God the things that are God's became no less a fundamental doctrine in early Christianity. Indeed, it was Jesus himself who enunciated it (Mark 12:17; cf. Matthew 22:21, Luke 20:25). Jesus did not call on his followers to withhold tribute from Rome, nor did he call on them to overthrow Roman rule by force. God, not man, would usher in the kingdom. *Jesus, like the Scribes-Pharisees, adhered to the doctrine of the two realms throughout his entire earthly life.* And his followers likewise adhered. For once it became evident that Jesus' second coming was to be delayed, the early Christians pleaded with Rome to extend to them the same religious autonomy it had extended to the Jews. As long as the emperor did not obstruct Christians from believing that their Lord and Master had risen from the dead, and as long as they did not prohibit the peaceful spreading of the good news among the Jews and pagans of the empire, Christian leaders were willing to urge their followers to pray for the welfare of the emperor, even as the Jews offered sacrifices and prayers for his well-being. The problem for the early Christians was not their unwillingness to make such a compact, but the emperor's unwillingness. When that willingness eventually was forthcoming from Constantine, Christian leaders responded with swiftness and relief.

And the reason? The very same that had motivated the Sadducees, the Scribes-Pharisees, and the

Essenes. The Christians were *the* people of Christ. They were the true Israel, a people who, like the people of Israel, were sustained not by might or by power, but by the Spirit of God. They were a people sojourning in this vale of tears while longing for the eternal life that awaited them beyond the grave. Even when the Church became a worldly power, it never ceased preaching the good news that each Christian would find true salvation in the bosom of Christ—not in the bosom of king or emperor.

When therefore the Scribes-Pharisees sought to preserve the people of God by setting aside Caesar's turf for Caesar and God's turf for God, they were pointing the way for the Christians to come. *And just as the Scribes-Pharisees were wary of charismatics and would-be messiahs lest their visions unleash violent consequences, so the Christian leaders proved to be wary when this or that individual announced the second coming of Christ.* There was this difference, however: The Scribes-Pharisees could voice their concern, but they had no coercive power, for the state in Jesus' day was not a "Jewish" state as the states of the Middle Ages were "Christian" states. Only the procurator or the procurator-appointed high priest and his sanhedrin could judge the potential danger inherent in the teachings of a charismatic, order his arrest, bring him to trial, and render a judgment. And the procurator had the right to make the final decision as to that charismatic's fate. From perceived threat until final judgment, political factors alone weighed in the balance. Whatever link there may have been between the Scribes-Pharisees and the political authorities, it was a link that derived from the doctrine of the two realms, not a link that derived from Jesus' "heretical" teachings.

If, then, we are to assess responsibility, we once again find ourselves laying it at the feet of the Roman imperial system, a system which had made the doctrine of the two realms necessary for the survival of Judaism. The times were no ordinary times; the tempests, no ordinary tempests; the bedlam, no ordinary bedlam; the derangements, no ordinary derangements. The chaos that gave birth to a charismatic like Jesus was the very chaos that rendered clarity of judgment impossible. The Roman emperor held the life or death of the Jewish people in the palm of his hand; the procurator's sword was always at the ready; the high priest's eyes were always penetrating and his ears always keen; the soldiery was always eager for the slaughter. Jewish religious leaders stumbled dazed from day to day, not knowing what they should do or not do, say or not say, urge or not urge. Everyone was entangled within a web of circumstance from which there was no way out. Whatever one did was wrong; whatever one thought was belied; whatever one hoped for was betrayed. Thrashing about in a world gone berserk, and in abysmal ignorance of the outcome of any decision or action, one did what, in one's human frailty, one thought was the right thing to do. The emperor sought to govern an empire; the procurator sought to hold anarchy in check; the high priest sought to hold on to his office; the members of the high priest's sanhedrin sought to spare the people the dangerous consequences of a charismatic's innocent visions of the kingdom of God, which they themselves believed was not really at hand; the Scribes-Pharisees sought to lift up the eyes of the people from the sufferings of this world to the peace of life eternal; the followers of Jesus sought to make sense of the confusion and terror which enveloped the last days of the life of their Master and Teacher.

It is in this maelstrom of time, place, and circumstance, in tandem with impulse-ridden, tempest-tossed, and blinded sons of men, that the tragedy of Jesus' crucifixion is to be found. It was not the Jewish people who crucified Jesus, and it was not the Roman people—it was the imperial system, a system which victimized the Jews, victimized the Romans, and victimized the Spirit of God.

And Jesus understood. Twisted in agony on the cross—that symbol of imperial Roman cruelty and ruthless disregard of the human spirit—Jesus lifted his head upward toward God and pleaded, "Father, forgive them; for they know not what they do" (Luke 23:34).